The Case of Anna Kavan

D.A. Callard

The Case of Anna Kavan

A Biography

Peter Owen • *London*

PETER OWEN PUBLISHERS
73 Kenway Road London SW5 0RE

First published in Great Britain 1992
© D.A. Callard 1992

A catalogue record for this book is available
from the British Library

ISBN 0–7206–0867–8

Printed and bound in Great Britain

Of all the liars the most arrogant are biographers, those who would have us believe, having surveyed a few boxes full of letters, diaries, bank statements and photographs, that they can play the recording angel and tell the truth about another human life.

A.N. Wilson, *Incline Our Hearts*

Contents

*

Illustrations

The illustrations listed above are reproduced by
courtesy of Mrs Rose Knox-Peebles, the McFarlin Library
at Tulsa, Oklahoma, and Mr Peter Owen.

Introduction and Acknowledgements

*

The person who called herself Anna Kavan did her aspirant biographers few favours. She destroyed nearly all her personal correspondence and all of her diaries except those covering an eighteen-month period. Even these were expurgated and contain an admission of falsification. She adopted a new name, a new birthdate, a new physical appearance and, it would seem, a new persona and literary style. This done, she set about spreading disinformation about the person she had once been and, often about the person she had become.'I was about to become the world's best-kept secret; one that would never be told. What a thrilling enigma for posterity I should be,' she wrote in an unpublished short story. Rhys Davies, who knew her longer and possibly better than anyone, was asked after her death to write her biography by her agent, David Higham. Davies refused, saying that even after thirty years of friendship he did not know enough.

This book does not pretend to be an authoritative account of Anna Kavan's life. Certain facts, of birth, marriages, divorces and death, of travel and whereabouts, are verifiable by objective documentation. Some come from her writings, almost all autobiographically based but never truly autobiographical, in which fact and fiction mingle. Others come from her conversations with her closest friends. But how much credence can be given to these? She was, in the words of Raymond Marriott, 'A living puzzle. . . . She cast doubts, she lied, she fabricated, she romanced, she spoke the truth, she was most honest. But where did it begin and where did it end?'

I have tried to dissociate fact from fantasy, using my own judgement and, dare I say it, intuition. The responsibility for any errors is therefore mine. That no personality is amenable to a single interpretation is a caveat which should be carried on the dust-jacket of every biography. In the case of Anna Kavan it should be written exceptionally large. During her life she used four names: Helen Woods, Helen Ferguson, Helen Edmonds and Anna Kavan. She published under the names of Helen Ferguson and Anna Kavan. At times in the text I write as if these were two different people. They were, for at some time around 1940 she became someone else.

My thanks are due to a number of individuals and institutions:

To Charles Burkhart, Cass Canfield Jr, Richard R. Centing, A.L. Davies, Colyn Davies, Priscilla Dorr, Ray Gordon, Francis King, Rose Knox-Peebles, The Earl of Mar and Kellie, Raymond Marriott, Anthony Perry, Stephen Spender, John Symonds and Fred Urquhart; to June Braybrooke, who first suggested the subject to me, to Alan Ross, for publishing in *The London Magazine* the article from which this book grew, and to Peter Owen, Kavan's publisher and mine, keeper of the flame.

To Sidney Huttner and the staff of the McFarlin Library at Tulsa, Oklahoma, to Cathy Henderson and the staff of the Humanities Research Center at Austin, Texas and to Philip Wyn Davies and the staff at the National Library of Wales, Aberystwyth.

To Dr David Jenkins, for providing information relating to the medical aspects of this story, and to John Hooley, for information and insights into the nature of addiction.

To the Rhys Davies Trust and the Authors' Foundation, for grant aid which enabled me to complete the project.

*Helen Woods/Helen Ferguson/
Helen Edmonds*

*

1

Where It Begins

*

Throughout much of the nineteenth century, and until the idyll was shattered by the First World War, Cannes was a favoured place of expatriation for the English moneyed class, a fact still celebrated in its Promenade des Anglais. Here, on 10th April 1901, in a house inappropriately called Les Délices, Helen Emily Woods was born.

Her father, Claude Charles Edward Woods, was a man of independent means who gave his occupation on her birth certificate as 'Gentleman'. His family owned a substantial estate in Northumberland: Holeyn Hall in Wylam, near Newcastle upon Tyne. Several of them had achieved some academic distinction, though there was said to be a trace of melancholia and morbidity in the family. At the age of thirty-five he had met and married a young girl of great beauty but no fortune called Helen Eliza Bright. Anna Kavan used to claim that she had been working on the estate as a cook's assistant, but this is unlikely since her background, though not wealthy, was even more intellectually distinguished than that of Claude Woods. She was the granddaughter of Dr Richard Bright, sometime physician to Queen Victoria and the discoverer of Bright's disease. Other members of the family held eminent positions throughout the learned professions, and the Brights were, like the Huxleys, one of the great Victorian intellectual dynasties.

Richard Bright's son, Dr C.G. Bright, was a physician who practised at Cannes, and one of his four daughters was the

mother of Helen Eliza Bright. There was a story, doubtless
cultivated by Helen Bright herself, that her father had been an
Austrian count. If so, his name was unrecorded on her birth
certificate: Helen Bright was illegitimate.

The intellectual inheritance of the Bright dynasty was
perhaps the greatest gift that Kavan felt her mother had
bequeathed her. She also seems to have felt that, in the case of
her mother, the Bright gene had skipped a generation. Helen
Bright had married Claude Woods young, and she was only
eighteen when her only daughter, Helen Emily Woods, was
born.

Helen Bright was an avid socialite who, by her fortuitous
marriage, had entered a world denied her by her illegitimate
and relatively penurious birth. The fact that her daughter was
born during the Cannes Festival must have particularly irked
her. The child was sent away soon after birth in the care of a
nurse. 'to a place where there was nothing but snow and ice'.
Anna Kavan later speculated that the nurse disliked the cold,
and that the transmission of this loathing through her milk
explained certain neurotic symptoms of her own. It is certain
that Kavan always hated the cold, and the rooms of her flat
were always overheated.

After some time with a wet-nurse, the child went to live
with her parents at a house called Churchill Court, in West
London. In retrospect there was an impression of abundance,
'my father was rich then', and there were parties, fine clothes
and a pet pony. She had a nurse called Sammy who is remembered as being quite severe, though Helen was 'a good child,
without any effort on my part . . . docile and clean in my
habits and more than a little timid, always very quiet. Mouse,
they called me'. She was allowed to visit her mother each
evening for ten minutes before dinner. 'I believe this was the
period when I felt more or less happy in my life . . . as if I
belonged there,' she would later write.

It was not to last long. When Helen was four her parents

went to America, leaving her with Sammy, who took her to live with relatives of hers in Pepper Street, Southwark, London. The tiny bungalow seemed small and mean after the opulence of Churchill Court and, once more, Helen felt lost. She was operated on for a perforated appendix, which turned out to be full of hairs from paintbrushes she would suck while painting. After this, her father came and took her and Sammy to New York, and thence to Rialto, California. Claude Woods, perhaps in an attempt to shore up a paternal inheritance which he seemed to be rapidly dissipating, had bought an orange grove. Kavan described it thus:

> We lived in two little wooden houses, small and
> unpretentious. It wasn't in the least like Churchill
> Court, in fact it couldn't have been more different.
> There was no village inn, no other houses at all. Only
> our two little one storey houses set in the midst of the
> orange trees growing neatly in rows. Some little
> distance away was the corral for the horses and mules,
> a stable and some shacks for the men working for us.
> These were always changing, sometimes Mexican,
> sometimes Chinese, sometimes Japanese. And there was
> a permanent houseboy called Omato. . . . There were
> no parties, no smart visitors to whom I could be shown
> off as a pretty doll.

Helen's spinster aunt, Lucy Woods, a sister of her father who had also lived at Les Délices, was living there also, and Kavan recalled that she had seen more of her than she had of her parents.

Again it was not to last. 'At age six, I was betrayed,' she wrote of her parents' decision to send her to a boarding-school. From then onwards her parents' 'disappeared', her father for ever. Helen spent the next seven years in American boarding-schools, and it began to dawn on her that not all parents treated their children as distantly as in her case. Though she must have seen her parents on occasion, she was often left in the school during the holidays when other children went home. Reacting against this off-handedness, she retreated into a fantasy world and developed acute shyness.

The eventual fate of Claude Woods is unclear. According to some of Kavan's accounts and the testimony of Raymond Marriott, he jumped overboard while on a ship bound for South America, when Helen was fourteen. The first she heard of his death was when her mother removed her from her American boarding-school and sent her to another school in Switzerland. The shock affected her profoundly:

> Though I'd hardly known my father, I had built a fantasy round him, believing that, when I was older, he would make me his companion and give me the affection I longed for. By dying he seemed deliberately to have destroyed this hope and condemned me to lifelong loneliness. Now I felt myself alone against the whole world, more than I'd ever been. . . . I couldn't forgive my father for abandoning me, or my mother for her indecent haste in putting him under the ground.

Helen was now completely dependent on her mother. She attended boarding-school in Lausanne, spending her holidays with her mother and assorted adults travelling, 'always living in hotels'. She retreated further into her fantasy world and was eventually sent back to England. Here, she went to a 'progressive' girls' school, Parsons Mead School in Ashtead, Surrey. Again this was unsuccessful. In *Let Me Alone* she suggests that the headmistress developed a crush on her, but that she was also unpopular with the girls of the school. The story 'Out and Away' from *Julia and the Bazooka* gives some flavour of her school-days:

'That girl's maladjusted,' I heard the umpire say as I passed. The word was popular with the staff that term. And I thought, maladjusted to what, for heaven's sake? To their stupid hateful school? I certainly hope I am.

I simply detested the place, loathed everything about it: the girls, the mistresses, the rules, the hideous uniform. I'd have run away if I'd had any money or anywhere to run to.

When Parsons Mead School was seen to be a failure, she was withdrawn and sent to Malvern Girls College. Here she was remembered as being shy and gawky but quite athletic; possibly a little tubercular. She made a friend there called Ann Ledbrook, perhaps the first friend she had made in her disjointed upbringing, and one who was to remain a friend for life. Again, when the other girls went home for the holidays, Helen was often left behind in the school.

During the latter half of her school career the First World War was being fought, an event that had little effect upon her. However, human mortality was thrown into sharp relief by the Spanish influenza epidemic of 1918, during which some of the girls at the school died. Ann Ledbrook's daughter, Rose Knox-Peebles, says that this left a lasting impression on her mother, as doubtless it did on Helen.

Loveless, lonely, and with the tragedy of her father's death casting a pall over everything, Helen Woods spent an unenviable childhood. Yet it was only a more extreme version of the childhoods endured by many of her social class in the late Victorian and Edwardian years. Few other cultures in history can have done so much to avoid human contact with their offspring, keeping them at a distance through nurses, nannies, governesses and tutors before they went on to boarding-schools. Even in the presence of their parents, the commonly observed dictum was that 'children should be seen and not heard'. Helen Woods evidently lacked the psychological

toughness to surmount the emotional privations of her upbringing: it is not too fanciful to suggest that the melancholia
which afflicted the Woods family had been passed on to her.
The experience was to blight her life irreparably. 'Many people have difficult childhoods,' Raymond Marriott commented.
'Some survive them and some don't. Anna didn't.'

Despite the miseries and dislocations of schooling, Helen
Woods was academically successful enough to be offered a
place at Oxford. However, the sudden manner of her father's
death meant that no financial independence, barring a small
trust fund, awaited her. She was entirely at her mother's
mercy and she, who had done so well in worldly terms without
much education, had other plans for her daughter.

2

Kavan into Dog Head

*

In her novel *Let Me Alone* (1930) Helen Ferguson prudently recast her mother as 'Aunt Lauretta', a woman who seems to have had all of the characteristics of Helen Eliza Bright. Helen Woods was portrayed as 'Anna-Marie Forrester' (the punning of the fictional name on 'Woods' hardly needs underlining), a girl who, after a miserable time at school, returns home with hopes of going up to Oxford.

In real life Helen returned from Malvern College to the Manor House, Earley, a village to the south-west of Reading, where her mother had set up court. It would seem that the same round of parties, dinners and social occasions continued as before. On her eighteenth birthday Helen was granted an allowance of £600 a year, a substantial sum in those days but not enough, so Helen thought, to see her through Oxford. Her mother seems to have had scant enthusiasm for the idea of higher education, perhaps since she had had none herself, and was clearly thinking in terms of 'a good match' for her daughter. She herself had married a much older man at eighteen, and had become rich through it. In *Let Me Alone* it becomes clear that 'Aunt Lauretta' has no intention of sending 'Anna' to Oxford, and this almost certainly parallels the situation of Helen Woods at Earley.

Beyond the realm of fiction, it is not clear how Donald Ferguson entered the social orbit of life at Earley. He claimed consanguinity with the Earl of Mar and Kellie, a Scottish branch of the aristocracy, but an inquiry to the present earl revealed that the family has no knowledge of him. Like Helen Bright's Austrian count, this was probably a piece of *folie de grandeur* on his part. His family seat and birthplace was Bovey Tracey in Devon and, though his father had been wealthy enough to follow the nebulous calling of 'gentleman', Donald Ferguson was employed as an engineer on the railways by the Colonial Administration in Burma. Anna Kavan once suggested to Rose Knox-Peebles that he had been one of her mother's cast-off lovers, and this is quite feasible, since Helen Bright, as her years advanced, developed a marked preference for younger men.

Whatever the case, the match was encouraged by the older woman. Helen, barely out of school, found herself courted by a man of the world, and one who dangled before her the tantalizing prospect of exotic travel and escape from her mother and the social round of Earley. Throughout her life at school she had been among women only, and her lack of contact with the adult world, except teachers and the distant patronizing of her mother's friends, must have contributed to a degree of immaturity, which is hinted at in the fiction. There was also the need, which exerted itself lifelong, for a father-figure to replace the one she had scarcely known. These are the only explanations for her strange decision to accept Donald Ferguson's proposal of marriage. There is no suggestion in her writing that she ever regarded him with anything more than amused tolerance, and even this was soon to evaporate.

The marriage took place at St Peter's Church, Earley, on 10th September 1920. Donald Harry Ferguson was thirty, and Helen Woods nineteen. In *Let Me Alone* Donald Ferguson is fictionalized as 'Matthew Kavan', and when Anna-Marie Forrester marries him, she becomes Anna Kavan, the fictional persona whose identity she was later to assume. 'Matthew Kavan' is depicted, here and elsewhere, as being 'twice her age', which was not strictly true, though it must have appeared so to a girl barely out of school.

The book describes a visit to the home of 'Matthew Kavan', which is depicted as poverty-stricken and ruled by drudgery. This is followed by a disastrous honeymoon in London, in which the sexually inexperienced 'Anna' fends off the unwelcome advances of her new husband. According to the fiction, it is not until the couple are in Burma that she finally submits to him. Later fictional depictions of this marriage draw an unflattering portrait of Donald Ferguson's lack of erotic finesse.

In real life they travelled via Ceylon to Rangoon by steamer, and from there to Mandalay by rail. Donald Ferguson worked at Maymyo, a small town some forty miles south-south-east of Mandalay, where he had a house quaintly called The Chestnuts, which was to be their home for the next few years. Helen Ferguson fictionalized the period in *Let Me Alone*, and Anna Kavan dealt with the same situation and events in *Who Are You?*, a novella first published in 1963. A comparison between the two accounts is indicative of the differences between the two personae.

Let Me Alone was the second novel published under the name of Helen Ferguson. Quite long, and conventionally written, it has something of the influence of D.H. Lawrence in its style. Its heroine is a proto-feminist of the modern school, primarily interested in personal independence, yet somehow inveigled into marrying a man she despises. When 'Matthew Kavan' proposes to her:

> She felt both astounded and indignant, as though he
> had in some unexpected way made her ridiculous. She
> had never even thought of marriage. She didn't in the
> least want to marry anybody. She wanted to go
> through life alone, in her own independent, detached
> fashion. The idea of being bound up with another
> person in such a relationship as marriage was hateful
> to her. And then, to marry a person like Matthew
> Kavan! Her very heart shuddered.

Matthew Kavan wears her down by persistence which, combined with continuous pressure from her Aunt Lauretta and
the vacuity of her social life at home, leads her to reconsider:

Anna began to think seriously about Matthew
Kavan. Perhaps she really had made a mistake in not
marrying him. At any rate it would have been an
adventure, a way out. An escape from the horrible
empty rush of the Blue Hills social existence, and the
horrible, vicious, fluttering persecution of Lauretta.
And surely with him she would have had some sort of
an independence.

In his absence, she found it difficult to recall what it
was about Kavan that was so distasteful to her. It was
hard to bring back to mind that feeling she had had of
vainly shouting at him through deadening wads of
incomprehension: the feeling of his unreality, his
strangely inhuman side. It was chiefly his shadowy
insentience which had repelled her. And now she could
not quite believe in it. It seemed that she must have
exaggerated it, to herself.

The marriage takes place, though Anna denies Matthew
Kavan what he would have seen as his conjugal rights. Eventually, in Burma, he achieves his objective, again by dogged
persistence. Anna, still in her teens, finds that the only social
life permitted to her is among the 'established, respectable
British matrons' at the local club. Social intercourse with the
Burmese is strictly forbidden except for the giving of orders.
The colonial men 'seemed to fall into one of two classes of
behaviour. Either they ignored the women entirely, passing
them over as though unaware of their existence, boorish to the
point of downright rudeness; or they were assiduously gallant,
flirtatious'.

Anna finds herself cast back into her familiar isolation and loneliness, but now with no prospect of escape. Near the house is a swamp, which comes to symbolize the nightmare which she feels her life has become:

> By day it was not so obvious. It was veiled by the bright sunshine: hidden beneath the strangeness, the unearthly beauty of the place. For it was beautiful. The marsh itself had beauty. The great, strange lake of swampy ground, mysterious with velvety patches of black ooze; the sinister, sudden gleams of iridescence, like glasses mirroring some magic sky; the succulent, emerald leaves, dangerous and poison-green; the piercing blueness of the small flowers. It had some half-evil glamour. But at night, when the darkness took it, it was a demon world.

And, at night, she is forced to submit to the unwelcome attentions of her despised husband, with whom no meaningful communication is possible. In desperation, she innocently befriends a young man called Whitaker until her husband's jealousy drives them apart. With horror, she comes to realize that she is pregnant.

There is a final dramatic scene in which, attempting to evade the attentions of Matthew Kavan, she rushes out into the monsoon rain. As a result, the child is lost. The novel ends with Anna awaiting the arrival of a girl-friend from England, secure in the knowledge that she has subjugated Matthew Kavan and that their marriage is effectively over.

Anna Kavan's *Who Are You?* covers the same set of events as the latter part of Helen Ferguson's *Let Me Alone*, though the story is retold in a far more lurid, impressionistic manner. 'Anna' is simply 'the girl' or 'his wife', as if to underline her loss of identity. Donald Ferguson/'Matthew Kavan' is called Mr Dog Head, a nickname given him by the Burmese. Mr Dog Head is a far darker figure than the bumbling Matthew

Kavan, given to extracting his conjugal rights by marital rape;
a sadistic and erratic whisky drinker who enjoys bludgeoning
rats to death with a tennis-racket. Unlike the account by
Helen Ferguson, Anna Kavan's book is short and written with
a precise verbal economy.

The leitmotiv of the swamp as a symbol of horror recurs, but
far more prominent are the birds who give the book its name:

> All day long, in the tamarinds behind the house, a
> tropical bird keeps repeating its monotonous cry, which
> consists of the same three inquiring notes. Who-are-
> you? Who-are-you? Who-are-you? Loud, flat, harsh
> and piercing, the repetitive cry bores its way through
> the ear-drums with the exasperating persistence of a
> machine that can't be switched off.

A social failure among the British community and regarded
with scarcely veiled hostility and contempt by her husband's
Muslim servant, the girl is befriended by 'Suède Boots', a
figure corresponding to the 'Whitaker' of *Let Me Alone*. Again
the friendship is quashed by her husband, but not before
'Suède Boots' has discerned her misery and encouraged her to
escape. Again there is a climax in the monsoon. Then, in the
words of one critic, 'with a sudden jar the needle sticks and a
portion of the action recurs, with a different conclusion'.

In neither conclusion is it revealed how 'Anna' escaped
from this ill-conceived marriage. It did not last long. She
records in a diary entry of 28th July 1926 that she could by
then hardly believe in Donald's existence. 'Almost four years
since we were living in the same house, practically three years
since a few minutes conversation at the Belgravia.' The marriage effectively ended in 1922, having lasted a mere two
years. It was, however, in the isolation of Burma that Helen
Ferguson first began to write, so she later told her friends, but
nothing of this period has survived.

Neither book alludes to the fact that there was a child of the union. Bryan Ferguson was born in 1922, and it may have been that the unhealthiness of the Burmese climate for a child and the rudimentary medical facilities available gave Helen Ferguson the excuse to return to England. Donald Ferguson seems to have accepted that the whole business had been a mistake, but it was one his wife never forgave him for making. He seems to have grown in her personal demonology as the marriage receded into the past, from the dogged, inept Matthew Kavan into the sinister, sadistic Mr Dog Head.

The events of the following years are unrecorded, either factually or fictionally. There may have been a joint business venture with a friend, which seems to have failed economically. There were periods in the Manor House at Earley, and others in the South of France. In all probability, the vapid social round from which she had attempted to escape was resumed to some degree. The twenties, a decade of experimentation in all fields, were gathering steam, and its intellectual ferment was accompanied by a corresponding hedonistic reaction to the austerity of the First World War. New ideas, new substances were abroad, and at some stage during these years Helen Ferguson was introduced to the submerged world of that decade's drug culture.

3

'A Clean White Powder'

*

In 1874 a British chemist synthesized diacetylmorphine from morphine. However, he lacked commercial backing, and it was not until 1898 that Heinrich Dreser, a chemist with the Bayer Company who had helped to develop its other wonder-drug, aspirin, resynthesized diacetylmorphine. This, Bayer began to distribute under the trade name of heroin, the hero-drug. It was initially marketed as a cough suppressant and, ironically, as a cure for morphine addiction, but the fact that it was even more habit-forming soon became apparent.

The prevalence of opiate use through all strata of society during the nineteenth century is well documented. What might be termed 'recreational' use of morphine was well established on both sides of the Atlantic by 1900. Largely confined to the medical profession, who were exposed to it, or to the wealthy, who could afford it, the practice attracted little attention from the authorities, since it created few social problems. The superior power of heroin was soon discovered by laboratories other than that of Bayer, and heroin quickly supplanted morphine among those who injected opiates for pleasure.

Concerned at increasing opiate addiction, the US Congress passed the Harrison Act in 1914, heavily taxing opiates as a means to restrict their distribution. Unfortunately they had not learned of the addictive property of heroin and failed to include it, with the result that heroin became the cheapest and most available opiate on the market, as well as being the most potent. Supply expanded to meet the vast demand, and it was not until 1924 that federal law criminalized heroin, by which time demand, and the means of production, were well in place.

Furthermore, in 1919 the Supreme Court had ruled that the Harrison Act forbade doctors to prescribe maintenance doses to addicts, many of whom had acquired their habits through medical prescription. So, from 1924 onward, all heroin production and consumption in the United States was effectively illegal and in the hands of the underworld.

In the United Kingdom, partly because of import controls and the First World War, there was an apparent decline in opiate use during the early decades of the twentieth century. That it was firmly entrenched among the upper classes is suggested by a story in *The Times* (29th July 1916), reporting that a Royal Proclamation had prohibited the traffic of cocaine and opium, 'which has become a scandal in London'. The *Times* went so far as to offer its readers a booklet on how to beat drug addiction.

The cessation of the war gave rise to a vast social and cultural upheaval. Black-market heroin penetrated wealthy, hedonistic circles, as well as more Bohemian milieux. In fashionable society close to the Prince of Wales the drug was peddled by Mr 'Brilliant' Chang, who boasted heroin of the highest purity. Eventually a government report on the problem was commissioned, and this was to lay the foundation of British policy for decades to come.

The 1926 Rolleston Committee took the view that addiction was an illness and not 'a mere form of vicious indulgence'. It recommended that maintenance doses should be prescribed to addicts, either with a view to eventual withdrawal or, if the addiction were incurable, to allow the addict to function with reasonable normality. This policy worked well and, though accurate figures are hard to come by, the number of registered addicts actually declined from around 700 in the mid-twenties to a low of 199 in 1947. In the years after the Second

World War, the entire British Drug Squad consisted of two detective sergeants attached to Scotland Yard. It was only during the fifties that numbers began to rise again, and it was not until the sixties that heroin addiction again became a matter of public concern. Behind these official statistics, a subterranean world of recreational users continued to flourish. The authorities, if they were aware, looked the other way. The problems were to come much later.

According to Raymond Marriott, Helen Ferguson first took cocaine, then opium, before progressing to heroin. She would often claim to have been introduced to drugs by a tennis coach, who had given her them to improve her serve during a tournament in the South of France. Since it is unlikely that heroin would improve anyone's serve, especially a first-time user, doubtless the drug given in this instance was cocaine.

It was in the years between her marriages that Helen Ferguson began to associate with racing drivers, and it was among them, according to Raymond Marriott, that she began to use heroin on a regular basis. This is the period described in the story 'World of Heroes', published in *Julia and the Bazooka*. Among the racing drivers she found a disregard for life and a hankering to live on the edge which mirrored her own death-wish:

> The race track justifies tendencies and behaviour which would be condemned as antisocial in other circumstances. Risks encountered nowhere else but in war are a commonplace of the racing drivers' existence. Knowing they may be killed any day, they live in a wartime atmosphere of recklessness, camaraderie and heightened perception. The contrast of their light-hearted audacity and their sombre, sinister, menacing background gave them a personal glamour I found irresistible. They were all attractive to me, heroes, the bravest men in the world. Vaguely, I realized that they

were also psychopaths, misfits, who played with death because they'd been unable to come to terms with life in the world. Their games could only end badly: few of them survived more than a few years. They were finished, anyhow, at thirty-five, when their reactions began to slow down, disqualifying them for the one thing they did so outstandingly well. They preferred to die before this happened.

It was deep-rooted nihilism and a sense that life is given meaning only by constant danger which drew her to both racing drivers and heroin use. Heroin users speak of the 'rush' after injection, at least in the early stages of use. The attempt to recapture it leads to increased dosages and addiction. By 1926, Helen Ferguson was already habituated, if not addicted, recording in her diary on 20th July the need to go walking to overcome her craving for drugs.

Drugs, principally heroin, were to remain an integral part of her life until her death, some forty years later. 'Perhaps some inkling of the reason why a person begins to take drugs can be traced in these stories,' Rhys Davies writes in his Introduction to *Julia and the Bazooka*. Her lonely childhood apart, another motive suggests itself; the despair which was never very far below the surface. The racing drivers, in their proximity to death, and heroin, with its proximity, both served as antidotes to an intolerable world. 'The world belongs to heartless people and to machines which can't give. Only the others, the heroes, know how to give. Out of their great generosity they gave me the truth, paid me the compliment of not lying to me,' she wrote of the drivers. In a body of work whose sentences vie for poignancy, her definition of the truth is perhaps the most bitter she wrote: 'Not one of them ever told me life was worth living.'

4

The Diary Years 1

*

Helen Ferguson spent the winter of 1925–6 in the South of France. Here, in the village of Sainte Maxime, some forty kilometres west of Cannes on the coast, she met a painter with whom she fell rapidly and violently in love.

Stuart Edmonds was the well-to-do son of a department store owner from Kingston-upon-Thames. He was married, with a son, but separated, a situation complicated by his family's Catholicism, and was travelling in the company of a mistress, Phyllis Morris. He too had a private income which permitted him to lead a leisured Bohemian existence and to devote himself entirely to painting. Helen Ferguson had yet to decide what she was going to do with her life.

Anna Kavan destroyed all of her diaries except those covering the period July 1926 to November 1927. These were a record, she later told Raymond Marriott, of 'the only time I was ever in love', and they also serve as a unique insight into her psychological state before it became too complicated by habitual drug use. The diary begins:

> Real life is a hateful and tiresome dream . . . yet how happy I might be with just a little happiness. I possess in the highest degree the art of making a little go a long way, and I am not affected by what affects other people. . . .
>
> I realise completely the hopeless nature of my character. And yet, I still have a certain conceit; I still

feel superior to the majority. This is curious. Perhaps I feel superior merely because I understand and analyse myself more than other people. . . .

It is the summer of 1926. Both she and Stuart Edmonds have returned to England. Her son, Bryan, is with a nurse in Apsley Guise, a village in Bedfordshire, and she is staying in a nearby hotel, seeing him occasionally. She is obsessed by Edmonds, writing that she is alive only when she is with him, and having to convince herself of his reality by looking at photographs of him.

Helen's relationship with her son is complicated by the fact that he is 'partly Donald', and she has to force herself to go and see him. When she does, Bryan shows her a photograph of Donald which his father had sent him. 'The effect on me was most violent. I had almost forgotten D's appearance. Looking at his face in the photograph gave me a shock like the impact of hundreds of vile recollections.' Days later she is still haunted by the image.

She is also taking drugs. 'The H [heroin] makes one's eyes beautiful. There is no doubt that I am attractive. I watched myself in the glass for a long time, which gave me pleasure.' She has already slashed her wrists once and is completely dependent on Edmonds as a reason to live. 'If S does not exist my life is intolerable and I shall kill myself.' Edmonds visits her on 16th July, and on the 19th she is visited by Phyllis Morris. It is the first time that the two have been on friendly terms since Helen supplanted her in Sainte Maxime. Phyllis is evidently attracted to Helen and comments that she has 'a perfect body'. Yet there are ominous signs of mental imperfection: 'I am much more abnormal; indeed, at times, I am really afraid of going mad.' On 20th July she records that she has to take a walk to overcome her craving for drugs. The walk is near-hallucinatory: 'This afternoon a curious thing happened to me. The reality of everything began to recede. I felt lonely and inaccessible and forgotten, and had a number of illusions, sometimes vivid and sometimes unreal. There were two sisters, one of whom talked about a river.'

She has not yet solved the problem of what to do with her life, and cannot decide whether to sing, write or paint. On the following day Edmonds comes, and he and Helen go to Bedford together. Edmonds objects to what he sees as Helen's 'passivity'. Alongside these other anxieties is the question of who is to have custody of her son. She cannot bear the thought of abandoning him to Donald Ferguson.

She next sees Edmonds on 26th July, writing afterwards: 'Why should I be the only person living to whom happiness is absolutely forbidden?' That evening she returns to London and stays in the Westway Hotel.

The next day Edmonds sees her again and says that if it were not for his father, who is threatening to cut off his allowance, he would risk everything and go away with her. But, she writes: ' . . . he does not realise – or pretends not to realise – how abnormal I am'. On Saturday the 31st, Helen, Edmonds and Phyllis Morris go to Oxford together, and Helen records that she was 'heavily drugged'. Tuesday, 3rd August: 'My ankle hurt me a lot and I took more drugs than usual. . . . I have to take so much now to have the least effect.' The next day she has a throat operation, which ruins her singing voice. She sinks into depression and on 6th August writes: 'I have so few friends and most people instinctively dislike me.' She traces her problems back to her mother, saying that she had a similar upbringing to that of Ernest in Samuel Butler's *The Way of All Flesh*:

> The same tyranny – emotional and 'will-shaking' – the same hypocritical cloaking of oppression under the pretence of protective affection. All the old Victorian methods of bullying seem to have been revived for my benefit. How much happier I might have been now if

mother had showed me a little more freedom of
thought – freedom, or rather, independence of action,
was forced on me by her attitude.

And yet, looking at the matter from her side, what
an amount of disappointment I must have caused her. I
would never allow our relationship to run on smoothly
even in my youngest period when I was most
completely under her domination, but was always
heaving up doubts and difficulties, and making a fuss
over something I should have taken calmly.

Stuart Edmonds visits, and tells her that she is taking too
many drugs. 'I cannot bear him to talk to me seriously like
that.' They spend the day pleasantly in Leamington. 'How
incredible it is that the devil should allow me such happiness
for any length of time.'

On Wednesday 15th Helen vows to take less drugs, and two
days later remarks that she has reduced her drug ration so
much that it will be easy for her to give up altogether. She is
still seeing Edmonds almost daily, but she begins to doubt the
future success of their relationship. After another visit to
Leamington on the 17th, she records that they made love after
driving. 'Curiously our usual position was reversed; I felt shy
and self-conscious while S seemed perfectly natural and at
ease.'

A major obstacle to their relationship was removed when,
on 18th August, Edmonds's divorce was decreed absolute.
The couple immediately set off for the South of France for a
month but, after a week of travelling, Helen began to suspect
that she was pregnant. Much of their time was spent procur-
ing an abortion and recovering from its after-effects. 'What a
miserable waste of happiness,' Helen recorded. Edmonds's
father, who appears to have played as overbearing a role in his
life as Helen's mother had in hers, was again threatening to
discontinue his allowance.

After their return on 26th September Edmonds tells her
that he cannot continue to see her because of his father's
disapproval. In desperation, she rings Phyllis Morris, but she
does not want to see her. Finally she turns to her mother, who
is at Earley with a male companion called Jim. Helen's mother
approves of Edmonds and is pleased by the possibility of an
impending marriage between the two. Helen, however, is
secretly planning suicide.

Any sense that the diary is more representative of the truth
than the autobiographical fictions is shattered by the entry for
27th September, in which Helen blithely announces that she
had been lying throughout the diary. She has never taken any
drugs except Cibas (a pain-killer) and she has not been pro-
miscuous: '. . . my *mind* is quite honest: it is my foul
imagination that destroys me'. Evidently the only entry in
which she is certainly lying is this one, possibly because
Edmonds is reading the diary or because she fears that her
mother may have read it. It indicates that her habitual lying,
which some friends of later life would ascribe to her addiction,
was firmly rooted long before the drug habit had taken hold.

There are more dark thoughts of suicide on the 28th, but by
2nd October she is thinking more positively about her future:
'There is one type of happiness which I have never experienced: I mean the happiness of "work"; the satisfaction which
is to be derived from being intensely occupied and from the
sense of achievement from having created something. I think
that, before I die I ought to try and experience that.'

She decides to cut herself off from the past and to take a
room in London. In a remarkable prefiguration of her life she
muses on the possibility of changing her name in order to
make the break more complete. Her mother, she comments,
has been kind, 'with a sort of un-intimate friendliness'.

The main problem facing her relationship with Edmonds is
his allowance, which his father, who thinks Helen 'wicked and
immoral', is threatening to discontinue. Helen is well aware of

Edmonds's weakness. 'I know he is not the type of person who can support or protect anyone else: he needs support and protection too much himself.'

On 5th October she goes to see Edmonds's father, who lays down his terms for their continued partnership. Edmonds was going to suggest that his father give him £200 or £300 a year and, if Helen could guarantee the same amount, he thought that he would consent to their being together. However, the father wants to know Helen's mother's income, which she cannot give 'because of the silence surrounding such matters at home', and then demands that Helen provide £2000 a year, which must also be used to support Stuart's son, John. He adds that he does not want his son to be cited as co-respondent in the divorce case which Donald Ferguson would bring. To Stuart Edmonds, their only hope is to deceive his father into thinking that he has resumed his affair with Phyllis Morris, so that he and Helen can meet secretly.

On 11th October Helen's mother makes the surprising suggestion that she should study art in Dresden. The next day Helen lunches with Gwen, Edmonds's sister, and the couple meet once more. Edmonds asks her if she has been taking cocaine, then tells her that he has no hope of ever living with her permanently.

'It seems suitable that this wretched book should end like this' is the final entry in this volume.

5

The Diary Years 2

*

On 13th October 1926 Helen confides to her diary that she is terrified of the prospect of attending Dresden Art School. 'I have an unhappy nature and there is something dark and incomprehensible about me which invites misfortune.' The next day, writing of Edmonds: 'The fact is, of course, that we are too temperamentally alike, we both need to lean, but neither of us is strong enough to support the other.' Nevertheless, she spends the night with him in the St Pancras Hotel.

On the 17th she decides to attend classes at the Central School of Art and goes to see Bernard Meninsky, who had taught Edmonds, to arrange this. Meninsky, a Ukrainian who had been brought to England as an infant was, in his time, a highly respected painter and is remembered as a teacher of charismatic force. The diary hints that he was attracted to Helen, and the attraction may have been mutual. By now she has informed Donald Ferguson that she is with Edmonds, but their relationship is still far from secure.

On 27th October she and Edmonds go to Heacham in Norfolk, where Edmonds's son John is to be looked after. Helen notes that he introduced her to his friends as 'Miss Morris', 'and didn't seem to think it of the slightest importance'. Later they make love. 'We each had one orgasm,' she observes clinically.

On Saturday 30th her diary records, for once, a piece of optimistic self-analysis:

I want to live a primitive, animal sort of life, with one chosen man who satisfies me physically and with whom I can talk nonsense, behave childishly or be silent just as I please. I want to sleep a long time, eat a lot, sit about in the sun and be sexual pretty often. I don't want anybody else at all. I don't want the bother of being friends with people and having to talk to them. I don't want emotional (or any other) excitements. I want to love and be desired and appreciated. I want to be comfortable and happy and at peace – (not all strung up and excited as I am now whenever I am happy). My tastes are not in the least cultured. I dislike most plays, all reviews, picture galleries and 'highbrow' music. I prefer not to change my clothes during the day; not to eat elaborately served meals; not to wash more than is absolutely necessary. I would rather go to bed than sit up and dance.

In fact I am an animal: a lazy, intelligent, unsociable animal.

This represents Helen in one of her 'up' moods, and is contradicted by the bulk of her diary entries. Perhaps because she was two different people in the space of one lifetime, the label 'schizophrenic' has been attached to Anna Kavan since her death. Her psychological condition in later years would become complicated by sustained drug use but, during the diary years, though a drug user, she could not be called an addict. There is no evidence that she ever suffered from clinical schizophrenia, nor was she ever diagnosed as such. The entries suggest, with their emotional lability, their alternations between feelings of identity loss on the one hand and superiority and the sort of Lawrencian nature worship of the above, a depressive condition, possibly with a manic element.

Three days after the above entry Helen records that she had a prolonged crying fit while in the company of Edmonds. He tells her that he will help her to commit suicide, if she is really determined to do so. On the following day the newly enrolled art student records: ' . . . what a pity it is that I'm not really interested in art'.

The affair with Edmonds continues. 5th November: 'He swore by the Mass never to marry any woman except me.' Yet, ten days later, 'he said that he couldn't live with me because he didn't trust me, and I had told him so many lies that he didn't know what sort of person I was'.

Helen's mother is in London, and Helen now has her own flat in Francis Street, Westminster. Her mother is exasperated and enumerates Helen's failures: medicine, writing, marriage. 'I am that most unpardonable creature, an intelligent failure.' But on 10th December: 'If Mother weren't in town I don't think I could bear my existence. She has been most awfully kind to me, taking me out nearly every day and giving me lots of presents.' Helen complains once more of a feeling of un-reality and of memory lapses: she seems to be suffering bouts of literal paranoia in which the world and inanimate objects appear threatening.

Apart from continued uncertainty about her relationship with Edmonds, the question of Donald Ferguson, to whom she was still married, remained unresolved. She came across a drawing of his and observed: 'How astounding to be mixed up with a person who takes life so seriously that he can't even see himself doing it. What will happen when he comes back? How will he behave about S?'

These questions were answered on 14th December: 'Donald wrote a note saying I would hear from his solicitors – so he is going to divorce me. I don't realise it – it seems entirely unimportant except that S is distressed at the thought of being co-respondent.' However, she is cheered by the fact that her mother 'quite approves' of Edmonds.

She lapses again into despair. 16th December: 'The Lord has made me this way with a damnable sort of strength so that

I can go on forever suffering and being tortured.'

On 30th December she records that she has taken a flat at Albany Mansions, where she will live with Edmonds. But five days later Edmonds goes away alone on a holiday to Switzerland, swearing, before he leaves, that he will marry, or at least live with, Helen. The final diary entry on 29th January 1927 records that he has been away for nearly a month. 'Always before I think I've hoped in my heart for happiness even when I was most despairing, but now I've almost stopped hoping.'

6

Adonis into Oblomov

*

Jonathan Cape published three novels in rapid succession
under the name of Helen Ferguson: *A Charmed Circle* and
The Dark Sisters in 1929, and *Let Me Alone* in 1930. The
effort of achieving such an output in such a small space of
time seems to suggest that, in the early years, the couple were
more or less static at the Albany Mansions flat. However,
Helen Ferguson did not produce another novel until 1935,
and the intervening years were taken up by a move to the
country followed by periods of extended travel; to the South
of France, the Italian Riviera and to Norway. Some of Helen's
paintings from this period still survive.

In the early thirties they bought a house called The Elms in
the Chiltern village of Bledlow Cross. The house was large and
well appointed, with an adjacent tower which was converted
to a studio, and the couple settled down to a period of crea-
tivity. Helen designed the house and began to breed bulldogs
while Edmonds, always the more jovial and gregarious of the
two, captained the local cricket team.

Curiously, no record exists of a marriage. Helen chose to
use the name of her detested first husband for her first novel in
1929, but in mid-1930 was issued a passport in the name of
Helen Edmonds. It is possible that a marriage was contracted
abroad, but it seems more likely that the arrangement was a
common-law one for, when the marriage ended, there is no
record of a divorce. Stuart Edmonds's father, who held
ambivalent feelings towards Helen, was a near-neighbour in

Buckinghamshire. Stuart was very much in thrall to him, and his sense of Catholic rectitude would have ruled out a second marriage.

There was also a child, of which little is known except that it was a girl and that it died in infancy. It was alluded to fictionally in some of Helen Ferguson's writing in a rather cold way, which seems to suggest a sense of relief on her part when it died. It was an area of life she suppressed, even to her closest friends. Rose Knox-Peebles recalls: 'I did hear something about a child that died, but no details.'

It was during these years that Helen met a man who was to develop into one of her closest friends in later life.

My first glimpse of her had been when she arrived with her equally personable second husband at the Lechlade fishing cottage he had lent to a mutual friend and myself. She was a young woman coming over the pretty bridge spanning the young Thames where a trout stream joined it and where swans came to be fed below a window of the stone cottage. . . . Later I saw her gambolling in Bledlow with her cherished bulldogs, animals that always seem to me to conquer a high-strung temperament of neurosis by sheer weighty power of muscle and flesh. She and her husband lived luxuriously in Bledlow. There were social exchanges, a country pond placidity, and the village cricket team as captained by Helen's generous husband. She painted in thick oils, wrote her well-controlled novels; she had a son by her first husband.

Such were the first impressions of the couple from the author, Rhys Davies. He told one researcher that they had met in 1930, but it must have been some years later than that. Davies was by then a critical rather than commercial success, the author of several novels and books of short stories set in his native Rhondda. Unusually for a male writer portraying such a male-dominated world, his fiction was generally written from a woman's viewpoint. He had left the Rhondda for London with the express aim of becoming a writer, a vocation he pursued with extraordinary determination until his death in 1978. His last published novel, *Honeysuckle Girl* (1975), is an examination of the collapse of the marriage of Helen and Stuart Edmonds, and is one of the main sources of objective information on the dark waters that ran below the outward tranquillity of life at Bledlow Cross.

Helen was still using heroin. She did not register with the Home Office and receive a subsistence dose from a doctor; instead she remained dependent on the vagaries of the black market, which must have meant numerous involuntary short withdrawals and a constant sense of insecurity. Edmonds knew of her drug use and, more and more, he grew dependent on that legal but equally dangerous palliative, alcohol.

The year 1935 saw the peak of Helen Ferguson's career. After some years of silence she published *A Stranger Still* to general critical approval and, later that year, exhibited her paintings at the prestigious Wertheim Gallery under the title 'Landscapes in Oil'.

> On the surface there seemed to be no reason why Helen Ferguson's life should not proceed along agreeable lines, though in company with her boisterously extrovert husband she could strike one as being antisocial, and there might be a marked detachment from awareness of others, except in her strange, glacial blue eyes, which missed nothing.

As Rhys Davies deduced, fundamental incompatibilities between husband and wife, which had been concealed in the first flush of romance, were in the shared ambition to work and live as artists now becoming apparent. Helen's aloofness did not sit well with Edmonds's sociability. Nor was she highly sexed, as Edmonds was, according to Davies, and as the marriage foundered she withdrew completely from conjugal relations.

Edmonds at this stage was no more than a 'weekend painter'. He had begun his career as a disciple of Cézanne but now painted what Rhys Davies described as 'furious abstracts'. Neither these nor his earlier style found any public favour. His wife was not only an esteemed novelist but also a painter who had achieved a major show. Edmonds's only validation as an artist was his own belief in his ability, and clearly this was fading fast. He had never held a job of any substance, had difficult relations with the wealthy father on whom he was materially dependent, had undergone in his Catholic family's eyes the stigma of divorce: all justifiable in his younger years by an artistic vocation which had now collapsed. His daughter had died at birth; his wife was a heroin addict, increasingly unsociable and increasingly sexually withdrawn. The only areas in which he could show some expertise were at cricket, drinking and philandering and, more and more, he turned to these for comfort.

Now he doesn't work at all any more. He's given up painting and all his other pursuits. Now the only thing he likes is to lie on a bed or sofa, doing absolutely nothing.

Then he was very particular about his appearance, fastidious. He had eighteen pairs of shoes and a fantastic number of elegant suits for all sorts of occasions and climates. His shirts, which he sometimes changed several times a day, were specially made by hand, with an embroidered monogram on the pocket. I don't mean that he dressed formally. In the country, he often wore the same sort of clothes as the local people, only his were always made by a famous tailor and never lost their style.

Now he lounges about all day in a dressing-gown, untidy, unshaved. When he does dress, his expensive clothes look as if they had been passed on by someone else, too tight for him, unpressed, stained with food, drink, ash, God knows what.

The first time I went out with him, I remember he wore a blue shirt and corduroy trousers as soft and as white as milk. He was very attractive then, very sexy. He wasn't exactly slim, but certainly not at all heavy, just muscular and solidly well-proportioned in the brown masculine Mediterranean way, with an aquiline profile and beautiful sea-coloured eyes set in long, long lashes.

Now he's put on weight and it doesn't suit him. It makes him look middle-aged, mediocre. His skin is still brown, but somehow it looks unhealthy, more like jaundice than sun-tan.

Outwardly, and in every other way, he's become totally unlike the man I married.

So Anna Kavan described her husband 'Oblomov' in a story, 'Now and Then', published posthumously in *Julia and the Bazooka*. The man is clearly Edmonds, whose alcoholism at one stage reached such severity that, according to Raymond Marriott, Helen had to revive him in the mornings by holding a glass of brandy to his lips. Drink does not seem to have overly affected his sex drive and, after Helen insisted on a separate bedroom, Rhys Davies recounts that he became openly and publicly unfaithful. Unfortunately the couple had chosen mutually incompatible drugs for their escapes for, while drink stimulates gregariousness, heroin exacerbated the social withdrawal of which Edmonds complained even in the earlier years of their involvement.

'Oblomov' features in several stories in *Julia and the Bazooka*, most tellingly in 'High in the Mountains'. A woman who has just taken a shot of heroin drives away from her house and her detested husband to the freedom of the snow-covered hills. She reflects on their various incompatibilities, including their choices of drugs:

> I think smoking and drinking are vices, disgusting habits, they're so offensive to everybody. The smell of stale smoke in our house is revolting, it clings to the curtains, the bedclothes, no matter how often they're washed. Smoke hangs inside the lampshades, turns the ceilings yellow. Then, when he drinks too much, he gets quarrelsome and aggressive, embarrasses people by stumbling about and making stupid remarks. What I do never affects anyone else. I don't behave in an embarrassing way. And a clean white powder is not repulsive; it looks pure, it glitters, the pure white crystals sparkle like snow.

The consciousness of her own abnormality, of her fundamentally anti-social nature and of her shattered childhood surfaces a couple of paragraphs later on in the story:

> I know I've got a death-wish. I've never enjoyed my life, I've never liked people. I love the mountains because they are the negation of life, indestructible, inhuman, untouchable, indifferent, as I want to be. Human beings are hateful; I loathe their ugly faces and messy emotions. I'd like to destroy them all. People have always been horrible to me; they've always rejected me and betrayed me. Not one of them has ever been kind. Not one single person has even attempted to understand me, to see things from my point of view. They've all been against me, ever since I can remember, even when I was six years old. What sort of human beings are these, who can be so inhuman to a

child of six? How can I help hating them all?
Sometimes they disgust me so much that I feel I can't
go on living among them – that I must escape from the
loathsome creatures swarming like maggots all over the
earth. In a desperate moment, I once said this to
Oblomov, who was horrified, shocked, utterly
unsympathetic. He looked at me as if I was a criminal,
he almost shuddered. 'Don't say such things! If anyone
heard you talking like that they'd think you were
insane. I suppose you realise that it's not normal. . . .'
Is it normal to stifle me as he does, so that I have to
rush out of the house before the walls close in and
crush me completely? It's he who compels me to drive
and drive, as I'm driving now, to save myself from
suffocation and from all the people I really can't stand.

While Stuart Edmonds's sexuality appears to have been
straightforward, that of his wife was more complex and mu-
table. Her first sexual experience with a man had been with a
husband whom she found repulsive, and this may have
coloured her attitude to sex lifelong. However, the diaries
suggest that she embraced the new sexual freedoms of the
twenties with some enthusiasm and some fairly frank entries
indicate that, at this stage, she was not frigid and was capable
of orgasm. In *Let Me Alone* the fictional 'Anna Kavan' has
several schoolgirl affairs with her own sex and, when she
leaves her husband, it is for another woman. The diaries hint
at a lesbian involvement with Phyllis Morris, and she told
Rhys Davies that she enjoyed sex only once, as a schoolgirl,
with another girl. Much later in her life, Peter Owen recalls
that a friend of his who had visited her came away with the
distinct impression that she was being set up for seduction. Rhys
Davies was convinced that she was not lesbian, and pointed out
that 'her indifference to women – and a few wooed her – could
be dismissive to the point of rude arrogance'.

One woman with whom she became friendly was Rose
Knox-Peebles, the daughter of her childhood friend, Ann
Ledbrook. After Rose had been married for six years, Anna
Kavan remarked to her that she couldn't understand how she
could stay married to the same man, as men bored her
quickly. 'I understood her to mean', added Mrs Knox-Peebles,
'that they bored her sexually.' She also implied to Rose that
she could be very sensual. To Rhys Davies, a confirmed
homosexual with no physical interest in Kavan, 'a lack of
sensuality in her was basic'.

Heroin characteristically supplants the sex drive, and Helen
was using it with increasing frequency as her marriage collapsed. This, combined with the decline of her husband from
Mediterranean Adonis to drunken Oblomov would account
for her electing for a celibate marriage. Edmonds took his
pleasure elsewhere and so, it seems, did Helen. 'Experimental', another of the stories in *Julia and the Bazooka*,
chronicles a cold, passionless infidelity with a young man by
Oblomov's wife: its purpose being, as the title implies, experimental rather than erotic.

According to the account given by Rhys Davies in *Honeysuckle Girl*, it was at this juncture that Helen's mother, who
was in England on a visit, was told of her daughter's addiction
by Edmonds. Together they decided that the best course of
action was for her to go to a London clinic for detoxification.
As with subsequent visits to these clinics, Helen's mother
picked up the bill.

Mrs Woods had remarried in the mid-thirties. She contracted a marriage of convenience with an immensely wealthy
South African called Hugh Tevis, who was many years her
junior. Described as a 'financier', he occupied a vast estate
called Monterey, in the Constantia suburb of Cape Town.
Tevis was homosexual; quite visibly so, dyed his hair plati-
num blond, and kept a harem of epicene young men about his
vast house. Propriety in South Africa, never a particularly

liberal society, demanded that he make some pretence of heterosexuality, and Mrs Woods was delighted to collude. The arrangement gave her a young, and apparently socially charming husband and access to quite unimaginable wealth. No restrictions seem to have been placed on her travels: when in London she occupied a suite which was permanently retained for her at Claridges.

The withdrawal was successful only briefly. In the late thirties it was effected by a gradual reduction of the drug ration while the patient underwent narcosis, usually under the influence of chloral. It was an unpleasant, and not particularly effective method of treatment. Psychotherapeutic techniques had not been evolved and the main function of the clinic was to lessen the discomfort of withdrawal. The first story in *Julia and the Bazooka*, called 'The Old Address', describes the sensation felt by an addict about to be discharged from a clinic. Her syringe is returned to her and she throws it away but, when the nurse has gone, she retrieves it from the waste-paper basket. Outside, she is struck by panic:

Demented, in utter frenzy, I rush madly up and down, hurl myself like a maniac into the traffic, bang my head with all my force against walls. Nothing changes. It makes no difference. The horror goes on just the same. It was enough that the world seemed to me vile and hateful for it to be so. And so it will remain, until I see it in a more favourable light – which means never.

So there's no end to my incarceration in this abominable disgusting world. . . . My thoughts go round in circles. Mad with despair, I can't remember or think any more. The terror of life imprisonment stupefies me, I feel it inside me like an intolerable pain. I only know that I must escape from this hell of hallucination and horror. I can't endure my atrocious prison a moment longer.

There's only one way of escape that I've ever
discovered, and needless to say I haven't forgotten that.
So now I wave my arm frantically at a passing taxi,
fall inside, and tell the man to drive to the old address.

Neither Helen Ferguson nor Anna Kavan ever wrote about
'the old address'; the source of illegal supplies, nor of the
mechanics of purchase and supply which usually loom large
in the literature of heroin addiction. Contrary to the usual
pattern of addiction, she had no known addict friends. That
her first attempt at detoxification failed so quickly indicates
the severity of her condition. To compound matters, it would
seem that Edmonds had decided that their relationship was
over, and he did not visit her at the clinic.

Faced with the apparent incurability of her addiction and
the break-up of her relationship with Edmonds, she attempted suicide. According to Raymond Marriott, she attempted suicide three times during the thirties. After this attempt,
which seems to have been accompanied by some kind of
breakdown, she again found herself in a clinic undergoing
narcosis, a treatment which was used on highly agitated
patients as well as addicts. There was a third detoxification,
this time in a Swiss sanatorium.

When narcosis and withdrawal were over, Helen Ferguson
had time to consider her life in the relative tranquillity of
convalescence. She came to accept the incurable nature of her
addiction and the fact that she could not survive without
using heroin as a crutch. At times in later years she would say
that heroin had 'saved my life and kept me from madness'. In
moments of despair she would regret ever having taken drugs,
and speculate as to whether a brain operation might cure her.
It depended on the vagaries of her mood. There would be
other periods of detoxification in clinics but these, according
to Raymond Marriott, were merely to regulate her habit when
it was getting out of control; never with the goal of permanent

abstinence. That there was an underlying neurosis which fuelled her addiction is clear from the diaries but, by the late thirties, years of heroin use make it impossible to differentiate between this and the effects of long-term addiction.

Marriage had failed her twice. The first marriage would seem to have been doomed from the start, but the union with Stuart Edmonds had given her a few years of happiness. Significantly these were when Edmonds was still following his vocation as a painter, the years when they lived as artist-nomads in Europe. The rot had set in when they attempted some approximation of bourgeois normality in Bledlow Cross. Travel was another escape from the burden of identity, and from having to fulfil a social role for which she was unsuited and which she resented. There would be no more marriages. She was fully aware of the fact that her own intractable nature was in part to blame for the failure. In *My Soul in China* (1975), a novella fictionalizing the aftermath of the break-up with Edmonds, here called 'Martin', the Australian friend of 'Kay' tells her:

'You use me as a psychological prop all the time. You feed on me emotionally. . . . Max called you a psychological gold-digger, and you're a parasite too. When he said what a mess you'd made of Martin I defended you and said that Martin must have been a mess to start with. But my Christ, I don't wonder now the poor bugger was finished. No one on earth could stand up to it. You'd ruin anyone's life.'

From this point on there would be, in the words of Rhys Davies, 'the fierce struggle to live alone'. And there was one more, supremely radical step.

'Any act which shatters one's existential field is a suicide, however temporary, and gives one the opportunity of a fresh start,' she was to write. Charles Burkhart, who knew both

Kavan and Hugh Tevis, her South African stepfather, always felt that she found him attractive. If so, this may have influenced her decision to dye her auburn hair to the same shade of blonde as his. Narcosis and hospitalization had reduced her frame to spectral thinness. As a final act of severance from the past, she took the name of Anna Kavan, her own fictional *alter ego*. In the future she would refer to 'the Helen Ferguson years' with an air of unreality. Helen Ferguson was dead. It would take some time but, in the space of a few years, the transformation was complete. Suicide had failed her as an escape from identity, and now she did the next best thing. She became someone else.

7

Helen Ferguson, Novelist

*

Helen Ferguson was fortunate in gaining Jonathan Cape as her publisher. Cape were very much an up-and-coming firm, the basis of whose fortunes had been laid by the addition of T.E. Lawrence to their list in the mid-twenties. Jonathan Cape himself was enthusiastic about Helen Ferguson's books, but his enthusiasm was not matched by their sales, and the final three of the six books published under this name were under the imprint of John Lane.

> Poor Jonathan Cape. Over a period of years he published my unsuccessful work. He did it because he believed in me as a writer. At last I did produce something really good, something quite out of the ordinary, if I say it myself. The preliminary reviews were first rate, everything seemed set for success. You've really brought it off this time, Jonathan said. Then the war started. That was the end of that.

The book alluded to here is *Asylum Piece*, the first under the name of Anna Kavan. This was published in 1940, when the 'phoney war' was just ending and actual hostilities beginning.

Rhys Davies refers to the Helen Ferguson novels as being 'conventional Home Counties' in execution. This is not strictly true for, though stylistically unexperimental, and featuring named characters who are not always identifiable as *alter egos* of the author, they are nevertheless shot through with a sense of darkness and oppression which foreshadows much of Anna Kavan's work.

It is interesting that the first two novels, *A Charmed Circle* (1929) and *The Dark Sisters* (1930), are both stories contrasting the fortunes of sisters. Olive and Beryl Deane in *A Charmed Circle*, set in the stifling Edwardian atmosphere of 1904, struggle to escape from the tyranny of the Old Vicarage which is their home, and where they are expected to remain passive and inert until a suitable match is made for them. Beryl, the younger and prettier sister, rebels and takes a job as a shop assistant to a London milliner. However her employer, Miss Aguilar, seeks domination, part spiritual and part sexual, over her. This encroachment on her inner life finally drives Beryl back to the Vicarage. There, her sister Olive, prone to depression and unable to break free from the Vicarage, has tried to escape by the socially prescribed route of marriage. The courtship fails and, at the end of the book, both sisters are back where they started. Yet there is hope, at least, for Beryl: 'She had done it before, Beryl thought, and because she had done it before, she knew she could do it again.' The *Times Literary Supplement*, in a not uncritical review, saw 'promise in the book' but considered that Helen Ferguson was too ambitious in her theme for a first novel. *Punch* also found the book to be flawed but promising: 'Cancel the allusions to extroverts and inhibitions and there is an eerie originality about her book's aloofness from normal and fashionably abnormal life. I feel she has found neither herself nor her *milieu*, though the pains she has taken here persuade me she may yet make use of both.'

The Dark Sisters is set in the London of the twenties, in a world in which the convulsions of the First World War, female emancipation and general social upheaval have made possible the life towards which Beryl Deane aspires. The sisters, Emerald and Karen, live an independent metropolitan life: Emerald as a successful but manipulative fashion model. Her younger sister Karen seems to be unmotivated and content to live in a fantasy world of her own making, so Emerald tries to engineer a match with a rich young man. It can hardly be coincidental that he is called 'Edmond'.

Just as Stuart Edmonds had complained about Helen Ferguson's passivity, so 'Edmond' in the novel objects to Karen's tendency to retreat into her dream-world:

> 'Why shouldn't I let my imagination run away with me?' she asked, in her curious drawl. 'If I prefer the dream to the reality, what does it matter? It is only I who am concerned in any case.'
>
> She laughed inwardly at the idea of his daring to question her secluded world. She did not take him seriously. But he was indignant and dispirited, without any consolation, infinitely removed from her detached contentment.
>
> 'You are not the only one concerned,' he complained bitterly. 'Do you think it is pleasant for your friends to feel that you are always miles away, thinking of something else? That they are of no importance to you?'
>
> 'I don't compel people to become my friends,' she replied, somewhat sarcastic.

As in *A Charmed Circle*, the novel seems to end with a return to the status quo. Emerald, afflicted by guilt, takes Karen back to London, where she can return to her imaginary life. However, the reader is left in no doubt that it is duty and not love that prompts the decision.

The *Times Literary Supplement* was again unenthusiastic:

> She is a novelist who obviously immensely enjoys the handling of words; the care, although not always the felicity, with which she chooses her adjectives and

adverbs is everywhere apparent, but, in the process of word-finding much of the vitality of her story is lost. . . . There is much conversation, some of it trite, some of it illuminating, and there is much evidence that Miss Ferguson can both observe and describe natural scenes, and the pity is that so much talent and ingenuity should be wasted on such trivial material.

In the same year *Let Me Alone*, a directly autobiographical reworking of Helen Ferguson's school-days and marriage, was published, and it was in this book that the fictional 'Anna Kavan' made her first appearance. When it was reissued in 1974 under the name of Anna Kavan, the reviewer in the *New Statesman* called it 'a pioneering effort for Women's Liberation'.

Then there was silence. After three novels in the space of two years Helen Ferguson ceased to publish, possibly because of the loss of her daughter, and the subsequent years of travel.

In 1935 the story of the fictional 'Anna Kavan' is continued in *A Stranger Still*. She has returned to London from Burma, then escapes to the South of France, where she meets and falls in love with 'Martin'. Though 'Martin' is clearly drawn from Stuart Edmonds, the affair in the novel ends, but is commemorated by a painting which 'Martin' executes. Once again at the end of the novel the heroine is alone, and we are returned to the status quo. As in *Let Me Alone*, Helen Ferguson unflatteringly portrays her mother as a fictional aunt, and the artistically inclined sister of 'Martin' may well be drawn from Gwen Edmonds, Stuart's sister. There is a sharp contrast between the bleak, realistic world of the London episodes which open and close the book, and the light, hedonistic interlude in the South of France, where the affair begins and ends. Reviewers seemed to like the book. The *Illustrated London News* commented: 'Helen Ferguson, whose books are always good, has done nothing better than *A Stranger Still*.

She sees people very clearly; she sees women through their pretty skins and turns them inside out. *A Stranger Still* is a complete drama in which every actor is fitted out with a significant part.' This approval was echoed by the *Sunday Times*: 'It lives from start to finish. . . . The theme of the book is the essential solitude of the individual. It engages the mind uncompromisingly, and its style is well knit.' The book was recommended by the Book Society.

The following year saw the publication of *Goose Cross*, a mysterious fantasy novel set in a Chilterns village not dissimilar to Bledlow Cross. Quite unlike Helen Ferguson's other books, it is meticulously plotted and has affinities with John Cowper Powys in the way that landscape and history are seen to affect the present. Some manner of purgative curse descends upon the village at the end of summer, brought about, it is suggested, by the discovery of a Roman skeleton. Judith Spender is trying to save her marriage to Thomas Spender, the captain of the local cricket team, an insanely jealous man who is rapidly descending into alcoholism. Again paralleling real life, the couple breed bulldogs. When the curse eventually lifts, those who have survived the purgation emerge more whole. Critical response ranged from the guarded to the unenthusiastic. The *Times Literary Supplement* bemoaned the lack of plot. 'In fairness to her, however, it is necessary to add that she writes with considerable force, has a powerful imagination and . . . a wide range of language. Those readers who have a taste for plumbing the "death-dark universe" will find here material to their liking.' The *London Mercury* noted that 'Miss Ferguson draws on most of the literary conventions of the modern English country novel. Cosmic awareness, the sub-life of inanimate objects and mysterious influences of haunted pools appear intermittently. Nevertheless, the three dozen or so characters whom she keeps on the move excite interest.'

Rich Get Rich (1937), Helen Ferguson's last novel, is the

story of Swithin Chance, a drifter through life who believes
that he has a destiny to fulfil. He works with the mentally ill,
marries a rich woman, divorces her, then becomes a tutor,
vainly trying to discover his purpose in life. Then he encoun-
ters an old school-friend who runs a leftist bookshop and
becomes drawn to his sister, Mary, who helps with the shop.
He decides to drop out from society and to live as Thoreau
had done, as self-sufficiently as possible in a cottage where he
will write up his experiences. He grows closer to Mary, but her
brother is a revolutionary leftist who does not eschew violence
and he seeks to co-opt Swithin into his group. Swithin de-
clines, believing that the artist should be apolitical, and eventually dies in an accident. The novel was hardly noticed,
though received faint praise from *The Times Literary Supplement*: 'The story of Swithin Chance, who has a romantic and
unreal air for all that is related soberly and with quiet confid-
ence. Swithin had high ideals, a sensitive soul and a great
desire to be rich and therefore immune from the squalid
struggle of life. Destiny, unkind at first, resolved his problem.'

Rich Get Rich marked the end of the literary career of Helen
Ferguson. Her novels were good novels of their time, modestly
well reviewed and with modest sales. Their main interest to
the contemporary reader is as a chart of the development of
Helen Ferguson, in their symbolic rendering of her life and
experiences, and in the way they gesture towards the person
she was to become. Shortly after the publication of *Rich Get
Rich* Helen Ferguson suffered the most serious mental breakdown of her life. When she emerged from the other side, Helen
Ferguson, author, and Helen Woods Edmonds, wife of Stuart,
ceased to exist. In 1926, when close to breaking-point, she
had speculated in her diary about the possibility of cutting
herself off from her past, abandoning her friends and changing her name. The initial success of her relationship with
Edmonds, and the discovery that her vocation lay in literature, with painting as a second string, had rendered this

drastic move unnecessary at the time. In 1938, when she emerged from her second period of hospitalization in a sanatorium, she took the first steps to becoming someone else. Taking the name of the heroine of two of her novels, she became her own fictional creation and set about, wilfully, to destroy the vestiges of the person she had once been.

8

Ferguson into Kavan

*

When Helen Ferguson concocted the name 'Anna Kavan' for
the heroine of her 1930 novel *Let Me Alone*, it is highly
unlikely that she had ever heard of Franz Kafka. She knew no
German and *The Castle*, the first book of his to be translated
into English, was only published in that same year. Kavan is a
Czech name, but it can also be Irish, a variant on the more
common spelling of Cavan, after the county of that name. Its
choice may have been an oblique reference to the non-English
ancestry claimed by Donald Ferguson, the model for Matthew
Kavan. However, Anna Kavan had certainly read and
absorbed Kafka by the late thirties, and the fortuitous choice
of a name beginning with K for her fictional *alter ego* may
have been a factor in her adoption of that name in 1939. 'Why
does the K sound in a name symbolise the struggle of those
who try to make themselves at home on a homeless border-
land?' she was to ask in 1948.

During the summer of 1938 she spent a second period in a
sanatorium. On her release she moved into a friend's flat in
Battersea, and contacted her old friend, Rhys Davies, who was
then living in Maida Vale:

> One day a letter arrived from her. We were both living
> in London, and when I kept the arranged meeting I
> failed to recognise the woman running to me from
> under the trees of one of those suburban estates of
> dwellings. Helen Ferguson had vanished. This spectral

woman, attenuated of body and face, a former
abundance of auburn hair shorn and changed to
metallic gold, thinned hands, restless, was so different
that my own need to readjust to her was a strain. She
had not long been discharged from her second period
in a hospital, and later I came to understand why she
called one of her Anna Kavan books *I Am Lazarus*. She
herself had returned from an abeyance of personality
in the shades. The Lazarus myth always attracted her.

Rhys Davies, whose novels were quite unlike those of Anna
Kavan, was to become her closest friend in the literary world.
He had undergone his own metamorphosis and, like her, had
decided to dedicate his life wholly to literature. He too had
been born in 1901, though some streak of vanity impelled him
to give 1903 as the year of his birth, the son of a small village
grocer in Clydach Vale, a tributary valley of the Rhondda.
Possessed of a remarkable single-mindedness, he had spurned
the traditional route of education as a way out of his social
position and had dropped out of school before matriculation,
determined to become a writer. He moved to London, where
he worked in a succession of gentlemen's outfitters, writing
poetry and voluminous plays without success until, one rainy
Sunday, he sat down and wrote three bleak, naturalistic
stories of Rhondda life. These appeared in *New Coterie* and
were later collected in a privately printed volume. A novel was
commissioned and written: *The Withered Root* was published
in 1927 and, on its royalties and an advance on a new novel,
he went to the South of France and befriended Lawrence at
the crucial time that the dying novelist was seeking publication of *Lady Chatterley's Lover*. A highly closeted but confirmed homosexual from an early age, he lived intermittently
throughout the thirties with a man called Vincent Wells, the
wealthy director of a City brewing firm, and produced novels
and short stories at a prodigious rate, following no other

occupation but writing. His sole extravagance, almost to the point of dandyism, was a taste for expensive clothes and, though he owned very little but his wardrobe and battled continuously with poverty, it would have been difficult to recognize in the cultured, urbane habitué of the Café Royal the young, half-educated innocent who had come to London filled with unrealistic dreams of making his living as an author. Against all odds he had succeeded, and his *embourgeoisement* had been complete.

Rhys Davies is the R in the *Asylum Piece* story, 'The Summons', of whom Anna Kavan wrote: 'I still felt that a close and indestructible understanding existed between R and myself: an understanding which had its roots in some fundamental character similarity and was therefore exempt from the accidents of change.' Aside from their mutual dedication to literature and their self-transformations, both had secret lives: Rhys Davies as a homosexual and Anna Kavan as an addict. It was not until after the publication of *Asylum Piece* that Davies learned of Anna's addiction. He recounts that 'The Summons' was based on an incident in the Café Royal, when he had been sitting with Anna and she had taken a dislike to an obtrusively hovering waiter. She had fled the table not, he later learned, to meet a mysterious stranger as happens in the story, but to give herself a shot of heroin. Just as the sensibility of an addict permeates and informs the work of Anna Kavan, so Rhys Davies's fiction, especially his later work, is shot through with a homosexual sensibility. Neither, at least in their lifetimes, dealt with their secret worlds directly in their fiction.

In 1940 Rhys Davies introduced Anna to an old friend of his, the theatre critic Raymond Marriott. Marriott was also homosexual and, together with Rhys Davies, eventually became her literary executor. As the freshly minted persona of Anna Kavan gained in substance over the years, she withdrew completely from heterosexual relations and her circle came to consist almost entirely of homosexual men, whom she would

sometimes use as a buffer to ward off unwelcome sexual
advances. According to Raymond Marriott, there were no
lovers, in the conventional sense, after the 1940s. She was still
an attractive woman and would remain so for many years, so
she was not immune from approaches by the more desperate
type of suitor. John Symonds recounts an incident at a party
during the fifties in which a young man, presumably in love
with her, took out his penis and pointed it at her. 'Put that
thing away,' she had snapped, apparently unperturbed.

Anna Kavan's first appearance in print was with the start-
lingly original *Asylum Piece*, brought out by Helen Ferguson's
old publisher, Jonathan Cape. She was one of the first English
writers, and certainly the first woman writer, to have absorbed
and transmuted the methods of Kafka: his depersonalization,
despair, and the constant struggle against anonymous, mysterious powers. The review that would have given her most
pleasure was praise from Kafka's translator, Edwin Muir, who
described her as a writer of 'unusual imaginative power'. The
book was widely praised, even by critics not normally associated with the avant-garde. L.P. Hartley dubbed her 'an artist
of great distinction', and, in *The Sunday Times*, Sir Desmond
MacCarthy wrote:

> If *Asylum Piece* is not based on actual experience it is
> certainly an astonishing achievement. . . . What is
> remarkable is that the subject of these stories not only
> kept the lamp alight in the fog of, at any rate,
> impending insanity, but was able to project
> dramatically the experience of fellow sufferers. That is
> just what the really insane can never do. . . . There is a
> beauty about these stories which has nothing to do
> with their pathological interest, and is the result of art.
> Two or three, if signed by a famous name, might rank
> among the story-teller's memorable achievements. There
> is beauty in the stillness of the author's ultimate despair.

The book was a critical, but not a commercial success. Money was not then uppermost in the mind of Anna Kavan, and news of the novel's good reception would have been delayed and must have seemed extremely remote. Before publication, as part of her quest for self-redefinition, Anna Kavan left England. She was not to return for almost three years.

Anna Kavan

*

9

The Wanderer

*

During the collapse of her marriage to Edmonds, Helen Ferguson became acquainted with a young New Zealander called Ian Hamilton. In *Honeysuckle Girl* Rhys Davies depicts him as a distant relation who is travelling in company with Mrs Tevis and who is seduced by Helen. There may well be some truth in this, as she was hardly in a psychologically fit state to make casual contacts with people at this stage.

Little is clear about the friendship, least of all whether they were actually lovers or not. He was much younger than she was, an Antipodean doing the customary world tour, apparently disappointed by the effeteness of Europe. He is 'the Australian' in *My Soul in China*, a novella that charts the collapse of Helen's marriage and its immediate aftermath. Written very shortly after the events it describes, it was eventually published, cut from 90,000 to 30,000 words in a posthumously edited volume. Here, 'Martin', a figure corresponding to Stuart Edmonds, is not the hopelessly alcoholic Oblomov of the later stories, but simply a beery, hearty cricketer with whom his wife Kay, recently released from a mental hospital, feels little in common. Reminiscent of her life with Donald Ferguson, Kavan made her fictional portrayals more dark and extreme with the passage of years. There is even an element of self-reproach in the story: an acknowledgement by 'Kay' that she is in part responsible for the state of affairs. But 'Kay's' soul has been in China, absent from her body, and she is haunted by the twin traumas of her breakdown and her drug withdrawal:

No, no, I mustn't think back to that time when I couldn't move because webs had grown from the backs of my arms and legs into the thing I lay on, and at implacable intervals the cruellest torturer of them all used to force down my throat the tube like a dead wet worm. (Through the centuries that I lay sickened by the nauseous stench of my cell, the loathsome stench issuing from my dead body, blown up by poison gases like a balloon; when in the darkness I shrieked with terror while jeering furies tormented and mocked me; when my throat burst and my eyes went out like rockets — where was the I that I can remember but am now no longer?)

Edmonds accepted the break-up of the marriage and in 1939 Helen, who had yet to begin her identity change, travelled to Norway, possibly accompanied by Ian Hamilton. Certainly he was with her when she set sail for California, where most of the events described in *My Soul in China* take place. On 25th January 1940 a UK passport was issued by the British consul at Los Angeles which bore this description: *Name of Bearer, Mrs Helen Edmonds; Maiden Name, Woods; Professionally known as Anna Kavan*. The transformation had begun. It has been stated that she effected it by deed poll, but there is no record in the deed poll registers of her having done so. Furthermore, the year 1940 has been given; this is patently impossible, since she was out of the country all that year.

She and Ian Hamilton occupied a beach cottage, he reading and relaxing, she attempting to pull together the shards of her life. She was still apparently taking drugs, and also drinking heavily. In *My Soul in China* 'Kay' comes to the conclusion that 'the Australian' cannot give her what she needs. She is to be thrown back, at last, on her own flimsy resources:

The dark region receded, all at once solitude took
control of the situation. Solitude had suddenly taken
possession of her, and of everything, stronger than
anything in the world. Solitude could even make her
forget the bad-smelling horror. Instantaneously she
forgot too how terrified she had been. The past didn't
matter; it was finished, except for the last slam of the
door. All that was left was the future, solitude, a new
condition of being with laws and circumstances as yet
unknown which would reveal themselves as she
advanced into it. She didn't know yet whether she'd be
able to bear this new state, but she could only go on
and see.

Anna Kavan, as she now considered herself, and Ian Hamilton, parted. He returned home to New Zealand. She took a
steamer across the Pacific and, on 29th June 1940, landed at
Surabaya, Indonesia. Her stay was brief and, on 10th July
1940, she landed at Singapore, where she was granted a
transit visa in order for her to change steamers for South
Africa. She planned to visit her mother and her new husband
for the first time.

That she did not was almost certainly the result of an
encounter with an affluent young American called Charles
Fuller. Like Edmonds, he was an alcoholic, and she was also
drinking heavily at this stage, a common by-product of heroin
withdrawal. Fuller was engaged to be married to a woman he
loved in New York and, somewhat to his remorse, in a
drunken state the couple had slept together. He is the anonymous American in the unpublished story, 'As Long as You
Realise'. The story is set in Java and in it, the man says that he
will 'look after' the narrator. He emphasizes, however, that he
is in love with someone else and is doing this because he
thinks the woman is 'a good person and a good writer'. 'I want
to take on a responsibility that isn't just one of the easy

financial sort I've taken before. . . . I'm not in the least in love with you. I'm doing this partly because I believe in you as a writer and a human being.' The narrator comments: 'It made me feel perfectly wonderful to think that I was going with him instead of to Africa after all.'

Anna recorded that, by 27th August 1940, a year since she had left England, 'I had crossed the North Sea and the Atlantic and the Pacific and the Celebes Sea and the Java Sea and part of the Indian Ocean. I had travelled about 25,000 miles, about the circumference of the world, in and between Norway and Sweden and America and Mexico and the East Indies.'

She and Fuller returned via Batavia. On 26th October she was admitted to New York for sixty days, and introduced to Charles Fuller's circle. They were Bohemian and artistic; she smoked marijuana with them, and was introduced to, and photographed by, Walker Evans. This is the photograph which appears – uncredited because its source was not known – on the jacket of most of Anna Kavan's books published in the UK. Fuller was about to be married, and the situation must have been ambiguous and complex. Anna Kavan was probably strongly attracted to him at this stage, but it was almost certainly the impending wedding that made her stay much shorter than the 'year' she later claimed it to have been. However, before she left, she made one important move towards establishing an American reputation.

That a glossy fashion magazine such as *Harper's Bazaar* should take to publishing serious fiction was the result of the efforts of a brilliant but eccentric editor named George Davis, who served as fiction editor from 1936 to 1941. Through his editorship it came to rival Harold Ross's *New Yorker* as a prestigious outlet for new writing, and on 1st March the Editor's Guest Book recounted:

Anna Kavan came to see us straight off a boat from
Bali. She had started for South Africa to join her

mother, then unpredictably turned about amid trip, drifted vaguely back to New York and appeared in our office, a blond blue-eyed young Englishwoman, book in hand. *Asylum Piece*, from which we have picked three chapters, was published in England in 1940 by Jonathan Cape. She wrote her first book in Burma at the age of twenty and has had six published since. We were not surprised to find that Miss Kavan had sailed for New Zealand before this issue went to press.

In late January 1941 Anna Kavan left New York on a steamer bound, via the Panama Canal, for New Zealand and Ian Hamilton. The complexities of her situation with Charles Fuller had been too much, and thereafter they saw one another only briefly. They remained correspondents, with Fuller sometimes sending her money when she was impoverished, until 1955 when there was an unexplained quarrel and he severed communications. In 1947 she described him to Raymond Marriott as 'the guy in New York to whom I'm quite attracted', and after the quarrel she wrote: 'I was attached to that young American. It's always sad to lose a friend (especially when you have so few as I).'

On 18th February she was granted a transit visa in Fiji and on the 21st arrived in Auckland, New Zealand, on what was to be the last stage of her wanderings. This was to be her home for twenty months; a strange choice since, at least in retrospect, she was antipathetic to much of New Zealand life and culture. 'It couldn't be myself, walking down Park Avenue, Takapuna, Auckland,' she wrote with some amazement.

En route she had completed and forwarded a novel, *Change the Name*, which Jonathan Cape published to a somewhat muted public response in 1941. From her Balinese sojourn came a somewhat unsatisfactory story, 'Department of Slight Confusion', which was anthologized in 1941 but never reprinted. In a mysterious biographical note she wrote that the author was in the process of becoming 'a new creation'. The transition into Anna Kavan was not achieved overnight. At this stage it was still more of a pseudonym than a realized identity and, for years to come, literary directories would point out that the author's real name was Helen Woods Edmonds.

She resumed living with Ian Hamilton at Takapuna, a small town in the North Island a short distance from Auckland. They lived there until September 1941, when they moved to Waitahanui, an even smaller and more remote village on the coast of the Bay of Plenty. The village, as described in a *Horizon* article, was primitive, isolated, devoid of facilities and with a backward-looking populace, 'haphazard collections of wooden bungalows, some incredibly dilapidated, some suburban-genteel, most of them with the appearance of having been knocked together by amateur carpenters at weekends'. Fishing and swimming provided the only recreations, though a game of tennis on a mud court was sometimes possible. Despite this they rented a house called Stratfield and Anna continued her process of self-integration.

She was as unimpressed by New Zealanders as Ian Hamilton had been by the British: at least in the view expressed in her 1943 *Horizon* article, 'New Zealand: Answer to an Inquiry'. 'The country itself is immensely more important than its inhabitants,' she commented, and she particularly disliked urban life.

> The city is indeterminate. It isn't England and it isn't anywhere else. It's null, it's dull, it's tepid, it's mediocre; the downunder of the spirit. . . . What you might call the leitmotif of all this is a quiet parochial slowness. People wander up and down the main streets staring into the windows of shops that are full of agricultural implements and meat pies. Everything's shut, there's nothing to do except go to the pub or the

cinema, or, if it happens to be the right day, to the
races. No music, no theatres, no pictures except an
occasional exhibition of local talent, no magazines of
what's termed cultural interest.

Anna was not in New Zealand for its people, nor for its
surprisingly radical political tradition, which she fails to mention at all. What attracted her was the relative absence of
population and the magnificence of the natural world:

Looking away from town life, the picture changes
again. There's a wide undetailed rough-in of empty
spaces, enormous tracts of green rolling country,
crumpled hill country scarred by erosion, nothing in
sight but sheep endlessly grazing, the homestead small
in its trees, remote and shut off in a life of its own,
grim perhaps, or idyllic, unimaginable really, a life that
seems to belong to a different era. And then the
beaches: with the lovely inexpressible melancholy of
the long sands, utterly desolate between dunes and the
greengage waves slowly unfurling. Nothing anywhere
except solitude and the sad shore bird's cry; absolutely
nothing but solitude, like a place that hasn't been
found yet and perhaps never will be found.

It is likely that a strong secondary motive in seeking this
isolation was an attempt to cure her heroin dependence.
Tentacles of supply would scarcely have extended to Waitahanui where, by her account, even obtaining alcohol posed a
problem. The main piece of writing to emerge from this period
was an account, barely fictionalized (if at all) of her travels
through the tropics. Entitled 'The Cactus Tree', it has never
been published, but is the source of a great deal of information on her wanderings. Not much else emerged from this
period except the *Horizon* piece and the stories 'Benjo' and

'The Gannets', which were published in the 1945 volume, *I Am Lazarus*. But a consciousness of the proximity of the polar ice-caps fills the *Horizon* article, and the desolate landscape may well have moulded the alien, vacant contours of *Ice*. Much of her time was spent renovating her dilapidated house, in solitary walks and exploration, and in photographing the native flora and fauna.

'The transmission of information is not my department. The only job for which I am qualified as an individualist and a subjective writer is the recording of my personal reactions,' she wrote in the article. For Anna Kavan, hell was not other people but a condition woven into the texture of the world. The nightmare might descend at any moment. In 'The Gannets' a woman is walking through a gannet colony when she sees the birds circle and attack a group of children, selecting and killing the weakest of their number. 'How did all this atrocious cruelty ever get into the world, that's what I often wonder? No one created it, no one invoked it: and no saint, no genius, no dictator, no millionaire, no, not God's son himself, is able to drive it out.' A visit to the gannet colony at Cape Kidnappers, on the west of North Island, generated this fantasy, which showed a precognitive vision of death by air: a vision about to become a reality in Anna Kavan's life.

10

The Horizon-tal Years

*

Little is known about the brief life of Anna Kavan's son, Bryan Ferguson, nor of the career of Donald Ferguson subsequent to the couple's separation. Ferguson was granted custody of Bryan after the divorce in 1927. Bryan was already spending most of his time with a nurse, and he would have been privately educated if his father had continued his work. That he frequently visited his mother is suggested by photographs in the Tulsa archive, yet she never wrote about him either factually or fictionally, except briefly in the diaries where she recalls, with some distaste, that he is, in part, her husband's child. As with her lost daughter, he did not seem to register on her psychological map. Much like her mother, she seems to have detested the process of childbirth, and once told Rose Knox-Peebles that she had undergone so many abortions that eventually she was unable to conceive. It is likely that Bryan's childhood was as lonely as had been that of Helen Woods, though there seems to have been more affection between child and parent than there had been in her case.

In 1942 Bryan Ferguson, who had joined the RAF at the beginning of the war, was reported missing in action after a bombing raid over Germany. When news reached Anna she was desperate to return to England and set out on three occasions, only to be turned back because of enemy submarine activity in the South Pacific. Problems were caused by the accident of her birth in France, and it was asserted on her passport that she was a 'British Citizen by Marriage', a rather too vague definition for those security-conscious times. On the fourth attempt she succeeded in getting a boat that travelled via the Panama Canal to Liverpool, which she reached on 25th January 1943. When she arrived in London a few days later it was clear that her son was missing, presumed dead. Poignantly, he had left the little he possessed in his will to the mother he had scarcely known.

She made a fresh suicide attempt and once again was admitted to a psychiatric hospital. Again she was treated by narcosis and, when she emerged from her long, drugged sleep, one of the first people she saw was the man who was to become her mentor and father-figure for the next two decades, Dr Karl Theodore Bluth.

Bluth was born in 1882 to a Prussian Protestant family, and had combined his medical career with his intellectual interests. He had written for and about the stage, and had authored a commentary on the aphorisms of Hardenberg, the German poet and novelist who had used the pseudonym Novalis. Bluth counted both Brecht and Heidegger among his friends, and his anti-fascist views had caused him to leave Germany in 1934. Married but childless, he worked as a medical consultant and psychiatrist and came to count a number of British poets and artists among his clientele. To Anna he was, 'the only one who ever made me feel as though I really mattered as an individual and as a person'. Dr Bluth must have become aware, as their relationship progressed, that he was going far beyond his professional duty in becoming the object of Anna's desire for a male figure who was part father, part lover, part mentor, but he seems to have accepted the role. It was Bluth who suggested to Anna that she should register with the Home Office as a heroin addict and, until his death, he was the source of all of her legally acquired heroin. Among his clients was Peter Watson, the wealthy aesthete who provided the financial backing for Cyril Connolly's influential magazine *Horizon*. Bluth himself was to contribute two articles to the magazine, and introduced Anna to Peter Watson, who accepted her impression of New Zealand for publication.

The fortuitous meeting of Dr Bluth and Anna Kavan was an almost perfect example of Emerson's Law of Spiritual Gravitation, which holds that people destined to do so will meet, apparently by chance, at precisely the right time. Anna's previous incarcerations in mental hospitals and sanatoriums had been nightmarish, and there had never been any attempt to get to the root of her disturbance. Anna felt a mystical closeness to Dr Bluth, of whom she wrote, in a book on which they collaborated: 'But the doctor who, I noticed, was watching me closely, said he felt between us the communion only experienced when two beings meet on the same existential field.' According to friends who knew them both the relationship was not sexual, though their closeness caused Bluth's wife, Theo, considerable anxiety over the years. The closest they came to sex, of a highly sublimated Freudian manner, was when Bluth administered her injections for her. He was the first doctor to realize the incurability of her addiction and the fact that heroin served as an antidote to her black, suicidal depressions. According to Raymond Marriott, all future detoxifications were undertaken, not with the goal of abstinence but to regulate a habit which had, for one reason or another, got out of control.

Perhaps it was a form of therapy suggested by Bluth that Anna worked for a while in a military psychiatric unit specializing in the psychological casualties of war. This experience inspired Anna's second article for *Horizon*. 'The Case of Bill Williams', published in May 1944. In his editorial Cyril Connolly introduced Anna as 'an expert on psychoanalytic methods'; an expertise derived both from her personal experiences and her work in the unit. 'Bill Williams' is an archetypal square peg in a round hole, a nonconformist in an institution, the British Army in wartime, which demands conformity.

Private Williams is a neurotic case. Society doesn't approve of Private Williams. The hospital staff takes a very poor view of him. Bill Williams is unpopular with the nurses, and the doctors are anxious to get him out of their wards. They say he has a bad influence on the other patients. They have no time for him because, in spite of pep talks and electrical treatment and benzedrine tablets, he persists in being resentful and unfriendly, apathetic and slovenly, unco-operative and bad-tempered, rebellious and disintegrated. Well, too little sleep, too much tension, too much danger, too much noise are apt to disintegrate some individuals after a time. That's the trouble, of course. Bill Williams is still obstinately hanging on to himself as an individual. If only they could get him to exchange his unsatisfactory, unstable, unkempt individuality with all its straggle of bits and pieces for a nice, neat, standardised dependable number, everyone's problems would be at an end.

Inevitably, right from the start, the social machine is the enemy of the individual Bill Williams. It limits the avenues of his mind, it trips his feet and lays traps for his fingernails and his tongue. Every door closing, every form filled in, every official broadcast, every regulation, every propaganda slogan, is a munition in the war; Society versus Bill Williams.

The article goes on to describe Bill Williams as 'one of the heroes of our time', who refuses to discard his neurosis and surrender to the machine. There is no hope. Anna suggests, 'unless neurosis becomes universal'.

Anna Kavan's piece was followed by a commentary from Dr Maxwell Jones, a well-known psychiatrist of a somewhat illiberal cast, who berates Anna for confusing individualism with neurosis, and puts forward a behaviourist solution to Bill Williams's dilemma. Perceptively, he concludes his piece:

'I suggest that the individual who feels stifled and restricted should not immediately blame his contacts. The fault may be in him. Frustration can be either a deterrent or a spur, as you make it.

Finally, I cannot avoid the suggestion that these remarks apply more directly to the creator of Bill Williams than to Bill Williams himself. Judged on the brief presentation of his character, he would be socially insignificant, and certainly far less articulate than Miss Kavan who has a remarkable knack of stimulating thought, even though her own attitude to the subject in hand seems unthought-out and over-emotional.'

The third part of 'The Case of Bill Williams' was written by Edward Glover, and is more sympathetic to Anna's viewpoint. Society, he suggests, is not a monolith but is composed of groups. Pertinently, especially in the case of Anna Kavan, he points out that 'the factors in both happiness and unhappiness lie deep in the recesses of the mind long before the adult makes his first acquaintance with social approbation'. He concludes that 'Miss Kavan . . . wins easily on points', but goes on to say that her mistake is to assume that the psychiatrist 'knows all the answers'. Earlier in the piece he points out that a society at war must, of necessity, curb individualism, and he ends his piece by suggesting that wartime psychiatrists should be retrained for the different needs of a society of peace. The article may have been a stimulus to Glover's *War, Sadism and Pacifism: Further Essays on Group Psychology*, published in 1947.

The pieces generated considerable controversy, including a letter to the editor beginning, 'I am Bill Williams', and an expression of outrage from Arthur Koestler, who also took offence at Anna Kavan's criticism of Mary McCarthy in the same issue.

Anna was now part of the *Horizon* group, perhaps the most influential then operating in English letters, and, over the coming years, she published a number of stories and reviews in the magazine. She was never, as has been claimed, 'assistant editor', though she did, at least once, describe herself thus in a letter. When asked in 1989 for his memories of her, Stephen Spender, one of the editors, said that he had never met her. On her own copy of *Ice* she deleted the words 'became assistant editor' from the dust-jacket, replacing them with 'started work at'. However, she did not amend the words 'in 1942', though this was a patent impossibility, since she was in New Zealand at that time. Her role in the magazine was principally that of book reviewer, and she seems to have been closest to Cyril Connolly, whose propensity for collecting around him young, attractive female aides has been much commented on.

Anna Kavan's reviews give some insight into her attitudes during this period. She felt that the genius of Virginia Woolf was not suited to the short-story form which 'is like a small room in which is concentrated a brilliant light, unfavourable to the binding of elaborate spells'. William Sansom, especially his excursions into 'that dangerous territory of dream symbolism where all laws are incomprehensible, all authorities incalculable; where the hidden threat feeds in every rose and all simplicity hides the ominous complication', found more favour. The review ended with a notice of James Agee's and Walker Evans's now classic volume, *Let Us Now Praise Famous Men*, a study in words and photography of three poor white Alabama families. Kavan had known, and been photographed by Walker Evans during her time in New York, as mentioned earlier, and that the book was later published in England may have been at least partly because of its sympathetic notice in such a distinguished forum. She wrote: 'It is

a terrifying fact that the post-war world will be full of damaged and helpless human beings with whose fate, if any values
are to survive, the whole human race must realise itself involved. Any representation, any experiment whatsoever which
will shock people into awareness of their responsibility to
these undefended ones is of supreme importance.'

Later in 1944 she reviewed two now-forgotten books, *The
Inquest* by Robert Neumann, and *The Power House* by Alex
Comfort. Both reviews, neither uncritical, served as sounding-
boards for personal expression rather than objective comment. Of Neumann she wrote:

> He does not realise that characters come fully alive
> only through the elucidation of subconscious tensions
> which determine the basic patterns of human
> behaviour. A writer must speak, as it were, the
> language of the subconscious before he can produce his
> best work. And this is true, not only of such writers as
> Kafka and James Joyce, who communicate by means of
> a dream or fantasy medium, but also of those who
> describe the external happenings of the outer world.
> Even in stories of action employing a realistic
> technique, the source of genuine interest springs from
> an understanding of the fundamentals of personality. It
> is the interpretation of complexes, together with their
> sequence of inevitable events which gives to any book
> the truly satisfactory rhythmic progression of music.

She praised *The Power House* because it stimulated con-
sideration of two vital issues:

> The first of these issues concerns the present-day
> tendency, to be formulated objectively as collectivism
> versus individualism. The word 'Collectivism' in our
> time has come to mean something more dangerous

than group living or group thinking: it includes the concept of the organisation of collective units into youth camps, labour camps and fascist conditions in general. A further extension confronts us with the mechanisation of social life; the machine versus the individual man, the wheel against the hyacinth of the heart. And, from a more subjective angle, there is the sadistic-masochistic trend which can be taken as the subconscious expression of the contemporary group soul.

Anna Kavan expresses ideas which had been common 'advanced' currency during the twenties, but which had been at something of a discount during the thirties, with their glorification of 'movement of Masses'. The ideas of Lawrence, demonstrably influential on the Helen Ferguson novels, are evident. So too is a heavy use of Freudian and analytical terminology. In her next review, her Lawrencian tendencies took a mystical flight which would not have shamed Lawrence himself. They also had special pertinence regarding her own 'detachment from the past'. Commenting on an essay by Woodrow Wyatt on post-war aims and values, in which he had written 'There are no fresh starts, no clean breaks, only continuations', she writes:

That is an attitude which fills me with alarm. I do not like at all the idea that a new life can be built up on the old foundations. As I see it, the new life must detach itself from the past completely, in the same way that a detached fragment of matter flies off from the sun to establish its own orbit. I do not like at all this talk of modifications. What is needed is not a modified past, an indecent mechanical imitation of something dead, but a blazing new sun, a creation wholly and dynamically new. Reconstruction is useless:

rejuvenation is useless: blood transfusions are no good
at all. What is wanted is a new earth and a new man
to inhabit the earth.

Such expressions were not unusual at that time, even in a
London suffering the full frenzy of the Blitz, when any future
at all was hypothetical. For a variety of reasons which remain
only partly explicable, a mood of experimentalism flourished
in the austere conditions of wartime London. Luridly named
groups such as New Apocalypse and the New Romantics
congregated in the *boîtes* of Soho, and there was a distinct
lack of enthusiasm among both writers and artists to treat
the war as subject-matter. The decampment of Auden and
Isherwood to America on the eve of war hardly served to
advance the Marxist cause which had been promulgated so
effectively in the thirties, and the nature of the war, fought on
so many fronts, often so mechanized that combat was remote
and impersonal, forced writers to turn away from wholesale
solutions to the human predicament into a deeply personalized mode of expression. Dylan Thomas supplanted Auden as
the voice characterizing English verse.

Reviewing Rosamond Lehmann's *The Ballad and the
Source*, Anna Kavan attacks what she interpreted as a common English tendency to confuse individualism with eccentricity;

Mrs Jardine, the heroine of the book, defines the word
'convention' as another name for the habits of society.
'When a habit is bad it should be broken,' she says,
and the greater part of her life is spent in disrupting
the conventional design on the acceptance of which the
comparative freedom of England largely depends. The
Englishman escapes tyranny because he accepts the
code of his class and shuns the danger of original
thought. Even if his conduct deviates from the

common formula the divergence is usually only a pseudo-individualism, an eccentricity, an exhibitionist quirk. His inmost self remains safely anchored in the traditional harbour. . . . Individualism, even of the imitation variety, is to the tradition-worshipping Englishman the modern sin at which he peeps from afar in horrified fascination.

With the ending of the war in 1945 came a relaxation in paper rationing. Paradoxically, rationing had been in part responsible for the experimental efflorescence of the war years, since more lenient regulations applied to magazines than to books. The result was a plethora of magazines and books that masqueraded as magazines, all of which fed a public starved of reading material. In her last review for *Horizon* in 1946, Anna observes that the increase in the paper quota had led, not to a continuation of experimentalism, but to a reprinting of Victorian classics. She always characterized her own upbringing as 'Victorian' and, commenting on this apparent regression, writes:

When laws, immemorially accepted as absolute, suddenly prove unstable as the wind, a collective human sense of insecurity becomes mobilised. The old gods have vanished; but neither Christ nor Quetzalcoatl comes to replace them. Confused, unable to understand a state of affairs so far beyond our experience and our development, we see only that things around us are changing, that the earth under our feet crumbles and falls away. In this terrifying situation we are all, whether consciously or not, in the greatest possible need of something which will stand firm: something which can be trusted not to turn one day into a shape of dread.
Only the most mature human beings can bear to

look our present reality in the face. For the survival of
the rest, some form of escape is an essential condition.
Humanity looks back in search of a sanctuary, because
to look in any other direction is to encounter the
treacherous unknown. Only the past is finite and, being
crystallised, cannot betray. We run away, so to speak,
backwards. This childish reaction of flight which has
become so general, demonstrates strikingly the
predominance of immaturity, and is at the back of the
craze for all forms of Victorianism. The structure of
the Victorian age could, in many of its aspects, be
described as a society of children: while we, escaping
into the nursery of that smug, self-confident era, are
ourselves the new Victorians.

Anna detected a general return to 'the ideology of the
nursery' in the post-war world which was just being born.
Characteristically she applies Freudian analysis to a sociological trend:

Psychologically speaking, love has been degraded from
the form-and-beauty fixation and reduced to the
possessive stage. The insistent craving for support and
comfort typifies the sedentary attitudes and posturings
characteristic of anal functions. Victorian life in its
entirety might, in fact, be regarded as a manifestation
of the anal complex operating on the group psyche.
The vampires and villains of the mystery stories; their
fears and horrors which never become real because at
any moment they can be banished; all these stem from
the sadistic aspect of the same infantile complex.

There was at least a germ of truth in this high-flown analysis, though it was to be some years before its effect was fully
realized. However, one by one, the little magazines engendered

by wartime withered and died, *Horizon* among them. Within a decade, a new wave of writers would look back on the period as one of freakish aberration.

But in 1945 the tide had not turned, and it was a particularly successful year for Anna Kavan. Her stories appeared in the *New Yorker* and *Harper's Bazaar* in the United States, and her second collection of stories, *I Am Lazarus*, was published to general acclaim by Jonathan Cape. The influential critic Desmond MacCarthy, a consistent supporter of Kavan's work, wrote in the *New Statesman* that,

> . . . one kind of fiction still fascinates me – that which deals with queer psychological experiences and describes the world in which people live who are mad, half-mad or criminals. . . . What is fascinating is to note as one reads both the differences and the resemblances between their experience and that of normal people; also the enormous significance to them of small details, which stand out with uncanny vividness.

The widespread critical success of the book combined with publication of stories in major magazines led the American publisher Doubleday to bring out both *Asylum Piece* and *I Am Lazarus* in a single volume, entitled *Asylum Piece*. Again this was critically well received.

In *I Am Lazarus* Anna drew on her own experience, and from her work with psychiatric war victims. One, who knew her personally rather than professionally, was Colyn Davies, a young man who had been invalided out of the army after a suicide attempt. Somewhat at a loose end, but with the vague idea of getting work as an actor, he had drifted into Soho, where he had met Anna's friend, Rhys Davies, in the Wheatsheaf pub. Davies was attracted to his younger namesake and for a number of years did his best to promote his career with

1. Helen Woods c. 1914

2. Helen Ferguson in Burma
   c. 1921

3. Bryan Ferguson with Mrs Ann
   Latch c. 1930

4. The Elms, Bledlow
   Cross

5. Helen and Stuart Edmonds
   c. 1932

6. Helen Edmonds
   with her aunt
   Lucy Woods and
   bulldog *c.* 1934

7. Anna Kavan and Peter Watson
   in Kreuzlingen, 1947

8. Anna Kavan and George
   Bullock in Davos, 1947

9. Anna Kavan with her mother in
   South Africa, 1947

10. Anna Kavan by Walker Evans

11. Anna Kavan with Dr Bluth in Kreuzlingen, 1947

12. Anna Kavan on publication of *Ice*, 1967

advice, friendship and financial assistance. His predicament naturally attracted Anna's attention, and she disastrously decided to cheer the young man up on his twenty-first birthday by taking him to see Walt Disney's *Fantasia*. The effect of Disney's occasionally sombre masterpiece was to send the still-unbalanced young man fleeing from the cinema in terror. 'It was the dancing elephants that finally did it,' he later confided.

Most of Anna Kavan's stories lack the leavening tragicomedy of this anecdote, and their bleakness coincides well with the mood of a country emerging from bombardment to post-war austerity and reconstruction. In one of the more striking stories, 'Glorious Boys', a Kavan figure meets a young bomber pilot, like her own dead son, at a party during the Blitz. The horror of war is palpable to her, 'the double stream of destruction, feeling the composite entity of the bomber-streams, gigantic cruising serpents of metal horror circling and smashing the world'. She asks him how he can bomb civilians, but her conclusion is one of war weariness rather than pacifism. She wishes that the war will end soon and, as the story closes, it is implied that it has, at least, for her. Another story, 'Benjo', deals with a strange figure who appears recurrently at her New Zealand house, wanting to buy it. She has no desire to sell, but 'Did he really know that I should be summoned away so soon, so finally, and in such lamentable circumstances?' News that her son was missing in action delivered the house into Benjo's hands.

Less personal and subjective than *Asylum Piece*, yet its equivalent in psychological insight into the shattered mind, *I Am Lazarus* established Anna Kavan in the vanguard of writers who had survived and assimilated the experience of war. The two books combined for American publication in one volume made an exceptionally strong début especially since, in a country grown immeasurably rich and powerful, there was a trend in publishing to seek out the writers who would

dominate the post-war world in the way that Hemingway and
Fitzgerald had previously done. It was possible in that overheated atmosphere to establish a sizeable reputation, as
Truman Capote did, on the basis of a few well-placed short
stories. Anna had published in the major outlets and her first
American book received critical acclaim and good sales. It
must have seemed that, having been pulled back from the
brink in 1943, she had rapidly consolidated her position and
that the literary success which had so long eluded her was
within her grasp.

11

A Language of Night

*

In publishing *Asylum Piece* in the United States, Doubleday had taken a contractual option on Anna Kavan's next book, and they published *The House of Sleep* in 1947, a year before the British edition. In this, Anna reverted to the intense subjectivity of her earliest work and sought to develop a 'night-time language' to express, semi-autobiographically, the nocturnal world of an unhappy child growing into adulthood. The book was resoundingly panned in America by most critics, with the magisterial Diana Trilling pronouncing it 'unreadable'. Poor sales ensued, and Doubleday cancelled their option on Anna Kavan's next book.

In Britain, Cape passed over the book and it was published by Cassell, who gave it an entirely unsuitable dust-jacket. British reviews were equally scathing and uncomprehending. *John O'London's Weekly* described the book as 'fascist', an unjustified rebuke which caused Raymond Marriott and others to write to the periodical in Kavan's defence. Marriott was a friend of Edith Sitwell, and in 1944 he had compiled an anthology called *Planet and Glow-worm: A Book for the Sleepless*. As Anna was a chronic insomniac he had given her a copy, and she had been struck by a passage from John Gower's *Ceise and Alcyone* entitled 'The House of Sleep', ending with the words 'And thus full of delight the god of sleep has his house.' *Sleep Has His House* was the title of the British edition. Sales in Britain were also poor, and Anna's literary career, so full of promise a few years earlier, ground to an abrupt and sustained halt.

During this time Anna was living, always alone, in Kensington, an area to which she remained faithful until her death. Now in possession of a regular legal supply of heroin prescribed (some have suggested, over-prescribed) by Bluth, she felt confident enough to visit her mother in South Africa in late 1946, leaving almost immediately for Switzerland. Here she spent some time at a sanatorium in Davros and, a month later, moved on to the Sanatorium Bellevue in Kreutzlingen. Her mother financed both these stays, though she seems to have expected some contribution from Anna. While at Davros Anna received the proofs of *The House of Sleep*, and looked forward with anticipation to its American publication for 'practically all the money I earn comes from the States'.

Anna had travelled out to Davros in the company of George Bullock, the lover and companion of Raymond Marriott. He had suffered for many years from a shrivelled lung, a condition that in 1957 proved fatal. Before the war, Marriott and Bullock had visited Somerset Maugham, and Maugham had contributed generously towards Bullock's medical expenses. He had ceased to do so during the war, angered that both men were conscientious objectors, but helped again in 1947. Anna's purpose in visiting Davros was to alleviate an active TB spot, but she did not find the treatment, given by a Dr Bauer, a friend of Bluth's, particularly effective, and she was far more interested in her psychological rather than physical ailments. Leaving George Bullock at Davros, she went on to Kreutzlingen where, under the guidance of Dr Ludwig Binswanger, a physician whom Bluth also knew and admired, she underwent detoxification. 'I haven't had a shot of anything for two weeks: pretty remarkable feeling after three and a half years of solid addiction,' she wrote to Marriott. However, she added:

I don't propose to keep it up for long once I leave here

and Binswanger doesn't expect me to either. But the
main thing is to keep it under control from now on so
that I don't deteriorate too fast. The thing about
Binswanger is that he's far more rational and
unprejudiced than any doctor except Bluth whom I've
ever met. He quite agrees that my depressions are too
hard to take without some alleviation.

In mid-April, Bluth surmounted various bureaucratic,
financial and marital obstacles and came out to Kreutzlingen,
just in time to cheer up Anna, who was in the depths of a
post-withdrawal depression. She and Bluth visited a number
of friends, including Martin Heidegger, around Zurich, and
they returned to London at the end of the month.

She remained in England for the summer of 1947, dealing
with her forthcoming book. In October she sailed to South
Africa, just as winter with its attendant depressions was
approaching.

The reputation of her immensely wealthy stepfather carried
with it a certain cachet, and in South Africa Anna found
herself being introduced as the 'daughter of *the* Hugh Tevis'.
Monterey, his mansion, she described as 'a cross between
Claridges and one of the smaller museums', where she had 'an
amazing gold four-poster bed in which to stay awake at
night'. She added: 'Staying with my mother is rather frightful
of course . . . this sort of pointless luxury somehow contrives
to make itself into a tyrannical machine, so that one is caught
up in a perpetual round of meals, drinks, changing one's
clothes and so on, and is never able to do anything one really
wants to do.' Yet, she admitted wryly, it had its fascinations:
'You know I have this existential passion for identifying myself with all sorts of peculiar life-forms.'

In November 1947 Anna wrote to Marriott from Great
Karoo, a dry plateau of semi-desert in the heart of Cape
Province. She was accompanied by Cass Canfield, the emi-

nent, wealthy New York publisher, with whom she had a close but platonic relationship which continued during her several visits to South Africa. The isolation of Great Karoo was much to her liking after the vapid social world of Monterey, and recalled the solitude of her time in New Zealand. 'It doesn't bother me because I'm so completely a non-gregarious being,' she wrote. She also mentioned that she had started 'my big existential novel'.

By 4th December she was back in Monterey and finding things difficult. 'It will certainly be impossible to cope with the situation here without the usual paraphernalia – much easier to obtain here, by the way.' She inquired whether Raymond Marriott had attended the funeral of Aleister Crowley, self-styled Beast of the Apocalypse, fellow-addict and slight acquaintance of both. Dr Bluth had apparently been ill and, on Christmas Day, Anna said that she would give him her income, if it would help.

Monterey was beginning to depress her. It was a vast house built in the style of early Dutch Cape architecture whose gardens were so large that they were eventually turned into a public park. Visitors were usually members of the South African and international *haute bourgeoisie*; wealthy British MPs wintering away and diamond mine-owners. The system of apartheid was relatively recent but it found an enthusiastic and lifelong supporter in Hugh Tevis, though not in Anna. On 21st January 1948 she wrote: ' . . . have dropped some heavyish bricks (mostly about the colour question)', and asked Raymond Marriott to help her find a flat in London. On 2nd February she stated that she found Monterey 'phoney, amoral and stifling' and described her fear of becoming caught in her mother's orbit:

I'm really terrified in a childish nightmare way of getting stuck out here, unable to move, and petrified forever in a repetition of my childhood isolation. It

must be bad for me psychologically to stay so long in
the neighbourhood of my mother. All the old
frustration paralysis feeling comes over me. I feel less
and less able to work or have any independent
existence – less and less a real person.

A concerted effort was being made to keep Anna in South
Africa. Hugh Tevis offered her a car and the use of one of his
cottages, Cass Canfield pressed her to stay and Helen Tevis
began to develop a series of neurotic symptoms, presumably
as psychological blackmail. It was no use. 'I begin to detest my
gold room where everything is arranged so perfectly for one's
comfort and yet it's just the smooth impersonal planning of a
perfectly equipped household where money is no object –
there's no real thought or friendliness in it, not a trace. No, I
should never have come here in the first place, least of all to
this luxurious mausoleum devoid of humanity.'

To compound her depression came news of the relative
critical and commercial failure of *Sleep Has His House*. On
22nd February she wrote to Marriott:

I am not in the habit of paying much attention to the
comments of reviewers; to do so on a regular basis
would surely drive one mad. Yet I can't help feeling
badly about the response to this one. For the first time
in my life I am unable to work and wonder if my
career as a writer is over. . . . For years I've depended
on my work as a *raison d'être*, but now that seems to
have gone down the drain. . . . One thing is certain, I
shall have to figure out something, for it is clear that I
shall never be a success at writing now.

She returned to London, sailing on 10th March and staying
for a while at the permanent suite which her mother main-
tained at Claridges. She had evidently resorted heavily to

what she had coyly termed 'the usual paraphernalia', for she left almost immediately for Dr Binswanger's sanatorium, where she underwent detoxification and treatment for abscessed legs, the result of carelessly inserted needles. She remained there for over a month, reading nothing but 'Kant, Kierkegaard and newspapers', the only bright spot being a visit from Peter Watson, the financial backer of *Horizon*.

For the remainder of the year Anna was occupied in collaborating with Bluth on a curious animal parable, *The Horse's Tale*. This was published in a small, semi-private edition, much of which was given away to friends, by Stefan Themerson's experimental Gaberbocchus Press in 1949. The book, whose equine hero Kathbar takes his name from an acronymic amalgam of Kavan with Karl Theodore Bluth, is a highly personal dream allegory. Kathbar is a circus horse and, at the end of the war, all circus horses are to be sent to the slaughterhouse. However, Kathbar is an exceptional horse who can sing and recite poetry. He runs away from his owner (significantly named Hugh), to become a celebrity in an artist's colony by founding a school of 'Hoofism'. When Kathbar learns that Hoofism is finished, he falls into depression. Yet, depression is never far from the surface of Kathbar's life. 'Life can't exist without the pull of annihilation,' he comments at one point. Again: 'It's amazing how people who refuse to accept death existentially are the very ones most apt to disseminate it in a factual way. You open up your arms to death and create a living process out of the pull of nothing. These others don't create anything, they simply kill.'

At a party held for him Kathbar becomes obstreperous and drunk, passes out and wakes up in an asylum, uncertain as to whether he is a man or a horse. 'I got the impression that it was not the hospital which existed for the benefit of the patients, but the patients whose function it was to provide the staff with an excuse for drawing their salaries. . . . It was a rule of the asylum to accede to every request made by an inmate, then simply ignore it.'

A 'Mr Patronage', a friend from the past, sends Kathbar to a 'mountain clinic', where a Dr Hieronymus tells him that his depression is due to a constitutional abnormality and that he is 'too gifted to lead the life of a horse'. Hieronymus, an *alter-ego* of Bluth, explains his 'existential psychology', Kathbar recovers his memory and sanity and returns to the circus.

The book is less important for its literary value than as an indicator of the close relationship between Dr Bluth and Anna Kavan. After a lifetime of alienation, she felt that someone understood her fully, at long last. In a letter to George Bullock in 1947 she wrote:

With regard to Bluth's attitude – one would have to write a psychological treatise to explain it. I think I understand his behaviour, but not the underlying cause of it. It's not that he objects to the idea of my going away – theoretically I believe he wants me to go – as I told you. But there is something in himself which preoccupies him to the exclusion of everything else. It's this preoccupation that on occasions cuts him off from reality and makes his conduct seem inexplicable and contradictory. He has been ill during the last week or so, and of course that increases the tension. I suppose I've been more intimate with him than other people during the two years that I've known him, so that I'm bound to be the target for aggressive manifestations which always attack those who are closest and most vunerable. The dual friend-patient relationship is inevitably hard to maintain and liable to misunderstanding. An additional difficulty is the hostility felt by Theo [Bluth's wife] towards me. She dislikes me intensely and is constantly trying, consciously or unconsciously, to make trouble.

Despite the difficulties of her previous visit to South Africa, Anna decided at her 1948 Christmas party to make her third visit there. It was not one she looked forward to. 'It is just simply and solely a financial expedient. Having unfortunately been brought up on a ridiculously high income level, I simply can't sink my standard of living below a certain point.' She was forced to deny to Raymond Marriott that there was any possibility of her marrying Cass Canfield who, 'never played anything but a ghostly part in my life'. Yet she conceded that Bluth had been jealous of him as Marriott would, on occasion, be jealous of Bluth. 'Please don't avoid him [Bluth],' Anna once had to advise Marriott, 'he loves talking to people and he likes you.'

Over the years, Anna's male, and almost entirely homosexual, circle acquired something of the atmosphere of a court, complete with infighting and competition for her attention. This was especially true in the case of George Bullock whom Anna once accused of confusing her with God. He was much younger than Anna and had also undergone psychiatric treatment; factors which she felt had led him to an unhealthy dependence on her. 'We are both, unfortunately, on the (sometimes subconscious) lookout for a parent-substitute,' she wrote. After she had left Bullock at Davros, she had written from Kreutzlingen:

> I don't believe there's any reason for you to fear
> damage from me, so that this anxiety to protect
> yourself in advance seems to indicate the existence of
> some deep-seated complex which it would certainly be
> unwise to disturb. Your dread of being put into an
> inferior position will disappear, I feel sure, as soon as
> you realise that inferiority and superiority are not
> concrete objects like chessmen, but only concepts inside
> your head. I suppose life can be turned into a kind of
> chessgame played for points, but that seems a very
> limited way of living.

This judgement with its authoritative, analytical manner could not have done much to allieviate Bullock's anxieties, and he was to remain always somewhat in awe of her.

Having decided to go to South Africa again, Anna underwent another period of detoxification. Her parlous finances ruled out Switzerland, and she entered the Greenway Nursing Home, 11 Fellowes Road, London NW3. It was the depth of a very cold winter and not a pleasant experience. Before entering the clinic she had written that, 'withdrawals are always terribly unpleasant, but in this country everything is about 90% worse than elsewhere because of the awful ugliness of both surroundings and atmosphere'.

The final stay in South Africa was brief, from mid-February to May 1949. It appears to have been as fraught as the others, and again she began to fret about her unsaleability. Raymond Marriott was an aspirant novelist and had just had a manuscript rejected. Kavan wrote from Monterey, commiserating:

Once I get back I'll need everything I've got – particularly as it doesn't look as if I'll ever sell any more of my work. How depressing. I'm sorry about Heath returning your MS. This is no world for serious writers. As so-called literature becomes more and more commercialised, 'real' writing is bound to take more and more obscure and personal forms until it's finally only intelligible to a small number of sensitive people. I suppose one must just be resigned to frustration and concentrate on the glittering prizes you speak of – not that I know what they are or where they may be found. Perhaps you'll tell me sometime.

Marriott eventually had some success as a novelist when his book *The Blazing Tower* was published by Quadrant Press. However, the career of Anna Kavan, novelist, was entering half a decade of total eclipse.

12

Eclipse and Renewal

*

Anna Kavan returned from South Africa to an immediate set of personal and financial crises. She had undertaken her journey there with the intention of saving money, as the amount of her allowance had never been increased and was being eroded by post-war inflation. Her mother would, on occasion, settle various medical bills and send cheques, but these served only to emphasize Anna's complete lack of independence.

Her first, and most serious quarrel was with Dr Bluth, who was angry about not having been paid for his services. His heart condition had worsened and, because of poor health, he was faced with the prospect of living on a much-diminished income. He poured out his frustration in a letter on 11th June 1949:

> I should give you some idea what is the matter with me. Theo has her own grievances; and my friends and main patients, whom I was able to help, hold again other strong opinions on you and your family's behaviour, especially after I have been crippled by my illness. . . . Apart from your stepfather's interview and politeness, I never had any answer from your family, with whom to reconcile you I have taken great trouble. . . . I beg you to settle what has been left unsettled. You must have some medical and psychological advice; but you must know that I have to

disappear completely: otherwise you would antagonise Dr. Backus (or whoever he be) on my account.

Almost simultaneously there was a falling-out with George Bullock and Raymond Marriott. It would seem that Anna, who had a strong influence on Bullock, had given him the idea that drug-taking might alleviate his poor physical and mental health. Anna was desperate, and wrote to George Bullock:

Honestly, I've no idea why no one remains my friend. I had (and still have) nothing but warmth and goodwill for you and Raymond, just as for Bluth. I've always tried to help you if there was a chance, and all three of you have told me at various times that I *was* helpful and that you were attached to me. Yet within the last few weeks all three of you have decided to cut me out of your lives completely; without any adequate explanation; without even taking the trouble to tell me personally what was the matter.

The crisis with Dr Bluth came to a head when Mrs Theophila Bluth took the step of writing to Mrs Tevis in South Africa. Mrs Bluth, known by Anna as 'The Tigress' or 'The Grimalkin', had no particular liking for her husband's demanding patient, and the feeling was reciprocated. The letter, of 9th August 1949, is also interesting in that it contains the only known medical diagnosis of Anna Kavan's psychological condition:

I wonder whether you would be kind enough to pay some attention to the fact that your daughter Miss Kavan has been unable to pay off her debts to my husband. She paid several instalments, and the last one in April '49, and has ceased to pay any instalments ever since. When your daughter was under my husband's care, she assured me that she would settle the matter 'as soon as she would not be so hard up'. And in the late summer 1944 Captain Maberley (on your behalf) insisted on my husband's continuing his treatment, although Dr. Bluth had suggested that the case should be passed on to Dr. Harris. These facts are confirmed by two letters from Captain M (the 2nd and 26th September 1944) and known both to Dr. Harris and Dr. Scott, who had assured Dr. Bluth that his fees would be paid by the patient's family. So I wonder whether you would ask one of your advisers to look after the matter and deal with it in a friendly way.

Miss Kavan was a case of obsessional suicide. After several revivals she had to be watched very carefully; for periods she had to be seen several times every day. Several withdrawals were given, continuous narcosis and psychoanalysis, and once Dr. Bluth was called upon to see the patient urgently in Dr. Binswanger's asylum in Switzerland. You will understand that Dr. Bluth feels hurt, if these facts are ignored, if he is not paid for his work, if letters he wrote to the patient's family are not answered. Nevertheless, in January '48 he had to help the patient again; he got in touch with the patient's present doctor and Dr. Backus. Some of the doctors have suggested that, for some psycho-pathological reasons, Miss Kavan would not pay her fees, even if she were in a position to do so. She probably would feel that I myself and my husband, who has given her valuable support, were no longer friendly disposed towards her. For this reason I have been extemely reluctant to deal with the case in a routine way.

Eventually both quarrels were smoothed over. Dr Bluth's bill was almost certainly settled by Mrs Tevis, since Anna had no money at all at that time. Ironically, all this occurred against the backdrop of publication of *The Horse's Tale*, the book that was to commemorate the spiritual identity of Dr Bluth and Anna Kavan. The misunderstanding with Raymond Marriott and George Bullock, who was now living in Porthcawl, a seaside resort, for the sake of his lungs, seems to have settled with the passage of time.

In order to supplement her diminishing income Anna went into partnership with an architect named Salmon early in 1950. The object of their firm, Kavan Properties, was to buy, refurbish and renovate houses, mostly in the Kensington area. The venture was a success, and it was to occupy Anna intermittenly for the rest of her life. She herself moved frequently, always remaining in Kensington; from The White House, formerly owned by Whistler, to 8 Kensington Court, from there to 27 Peel Street, thence to 47 Campbell Street and eventually to 99 Peel Street, where she remained for a number of years. Though the setting up of Kavan Properties occupied a great deal of her time and energy, she continued to write, though with little hope of publication. Her most productive hours were in the morning, and work might pass through half a dozen drafts. From initial notes, she would write out a first draft by hand then revise this in a second, handwritten draft. If this were satisfactory, it would be typed and a carbon copy made, both of which would again be amended. Then there might be a further typed version before a final draft was made.

Her life in these years was not reclusive, nor does she seem to have become seriously depressed. She frequently attended the theatre, often with Raymond Marriott, who had been promoted to assistant editor of *The Stage* and was thus the recipient of an inexhaustible supply of free tickets, Fred Urquhart, a Scottish writer who had been introduced to her by Rhys Davies, remembers seeing her from time to time in the Salisbury pub in St Martin's Lane. This establishment, with its mirror-decked interior, its rococo fittings replete with cherubim and its scarcely less ornate clientele, which might broadly be characterized as homosexual–theatrical, was much to her taste. She went with Urquhart to see Eliot's *The Family Reunion*, to which her reaction is unrecorded, and with Charles Burkhart to see a new play which may have indicated that the tide of literary fashion was, imperceptibly, flowing once more in her direction: Beckett's *Waiting for Godot*. 'We jumped on a big red bus to come home and she gave me a splendid smile and said, "I didn't understand it but I liked it very much,"' Burkhart recalls.

Burkhart's great friend, and a man who was to enjoy a somewhat stormy relationship with Anna Kavan, was the illustrious designer, Herman Schrijver. Schrijver had redecorated Monterey for Mr and Mrs Tevis in 1936 shortly after his most prestigious commission, the redesigning of Fort Belvedere for King Edward VIII. He included among his clients various Guinnesses, and a large slice of the wealthy aristocracy. A Dutch Jew, whose family had been obliterated in the Holocaust, he had begun his career as a shop clerk at £5 a week after his father, a diamond cutter and polisher, had lost all his money. By his own efforts he had raised himself to an exalted and lucrative position in London society, managing even to subsidize his parents during their lifetime. A wit, *bon vivant* and incorrigible homosexual, his florid style of decoration revolved heavily around *trompe-l'oeil* and an extensive use of mirrors, a detail that must have endeared him to Anna.

Anna was not his only friend in the world of literature. After the death of Margaret Jourdain, the friend and companion of Ivy Compton-Burnett, his talent as a raconteur of frequently heavily embroidered gossip led to his becoming Ivy Compton-Burnett's closest ally. At the other end of the behavioural spectrum he was also a great friend of the exhibitionist, alcoholic libertine, Nancy Cunard. Though they too quarrelled, Schrijver was fascinated by Anna and what he perceived as her 'witch-like' quality. 'Dinner at Anna's with Anna and Herman and me: restlessness increasing till about 8, then she went to her bedroom and gave herself a needle; and dinner and the rest of the evening were serene, rather remote, smiling,' Burkhart remembers.

In 1954 Kavan broke her silence and submitted a story, 'Happy Name', to *Encounter*. The story was printed but, otherwise, she was a figure from a barely remembered past. In a *Punch* article of the mid-fifties she was written about as if she were dead, and associated with the 'Horizon-tal heyday' of forties neo-romanticism. 'Happy Name' was certainly a retreat from the subjectivity of most of the forties' writing, and a more conventional style was to characterize nearly all of Anna Kavan's work during the fifties. Though it subtly explores the terrors of an old spinster through the medium of a dream in which she regresses to a childhood in a large Victorian house, Anna makes little attempt to develop further on the 'night-time language' of *Sleep Has His House*.

In 1955 Anna received word that her mother had died. Lifelong, her mother had been a spectre haunting her every action, delivering an implicit condemnatory judgement on whatever she tried to achieve. Her continued dependence on her for her allowance, her travels and her medical expenses served only to deepen the complexity of Anna's feelings for her. She was as dependent on the mother she despised as she was on heroin, and in neither case was severance possible. Herman Schrijver had once commented to Rhys Davies that, terrible though his parents' deaths had been, it was only after their death that he had felt truly free. This was not the case with Anna Kavan.

Mrs Tevis either died intestate, or willed her estate to her husband. Anna was to receive a share of the proceeds from the sale of the house at Earley, but she lost any statutory right to her allowance, though it would seem that this continued to be paid. She was in effect disinherited. It appears that Hugh

Tevis had suffered some kind of financial disaster. 'Herman always said that he lost a good deal of money in Rhodesia and that he was usually drunk,' Charles Burkhart recounts, adding: 'Some of both comments may have been true. Herman always exaggerated.' Whatever the case, Anna tried to contest the legacy, with no success. That she remained on terms of fairly distant friendliness with Hugh Tevis for the rest of her life might indicate that the story of financial reversal was true and there was, indeed, no money to be had.

A few things came her way: some miniatures and effects from the house at Earley, her mother's harp which, ever after, was a feature of her drawing-room, and a grotesquely idealized portrait of Mrs Tevis which, for reasons that none of Anna's friends could fathom, remained visibly on display. Rhys Davies remembers:

> After the death of Anna's mother, an opulent portrait
> of her hung prominently in the daughter's house.
> Lavish in oils and idealised execution, its bejewelled
> subject carried a sheaf of deadly white lilies, and a
> smooth face bore a hostess kind of charm. The
> painting hung over a dining table on which the
> daughter wrote her novels and short stories. Visitors
> could not fail to notice the dominant, if commonplace,
> portrait. Worldly and private success exuded from it.
> Accustomed to Anna's deepening bitterness towards her
> mother, to say nothing of her understanding of good
> painting, I sometimes wondered why she could tolerate
> the portrait there.
>
> One evening, glaring at it, she attacked its subject
> with such a depth of hostile repudiation that,
> accustomed to the sudden minor violence manifested
> occasionally at this particular hour, I expected a plate
> or wineglass to be hurled from the dining table.
> Presently she subsided. It was approaching 10 o'clock:

the hour of her evening escape. In her bedroom the palliative would be dissolved in a tiny jar, a syringe – her 'bazooka', she called it – filled, and its needle thrust into a thigh with the efficiency of long, long experience.

Charles Burkhart also recalls the 'hideous grand portrait of her mother which was always in the living-room', and where it must have looked odd among Anna's own modernist pieces and (until shortage of money forced her to sell it) a Graham Sutherland. It is some indication of Mrs Tevis's aesthetic taste that the portrait had been commissioned in 1950 from Vladimir Tretchikoff, the artist probably best known as creator of that most enduring icon of twentieth-century kitsch, the green-faced oriental girl.

During her life there would seem to have been a love-hate element in the relationship of Anna with her mother, but hatred predominated after her death. As an act of vengeance, Anna wrote *A Scarcity of Love*, a fantastic reworking of her relationship with her mother. She is depicted as 'Regina', a self-centred narcissist showing affinities with Hans Christian Andersen's Snow Queen. As in Andersen's story the object of her malevolence, her only daughter, is called Gerda. Regina detests both sex and childbirth: 'The other was bad enough – but this. . . . It's obscene, I tell you, this giving birth! A loathsome obscenity – now do you understand?' The child grows up unwanted and retreats into a world of fantasy, painfully shy and with only a nebulous sense of identity and self-worth. Unable to adapt to everyday human relationships, she finally drowns herself:

With sudden intensity, she longed to escape from all the sadness, the guilt and the not-being-loved, of the world to which she had come unwanted, where nobody wished her to stay.

She had a vague notion that she was to blame for her own unhappiness. But she no longer understood how this was so. She could no longer remember what she'd done wrong – the things left undone, unsaid. . . . It all seemed far away . . . long ago . . . not so very important. She knew she had always been stupid: there had always been so much she did not understand . . . and no one had ever explained. But now it seemed not to matter much any more.

Regina eventually marries a man many years younger than she and they live in a tropical 'earthly paradise'. But Regina cannot face the ageing of her own body and slips into a valetudinarian existence. Eventually, half-mad, she strikes the gardener's daughter, whom her husband has befriended, then dies. After her death the husband hears the child chanting: 'You're dead, old witch, and you can't come back . . . you're under the ground and you can't get out . . . you'll never get out again.' He is shocked, but the greatest shock comes with the reading of Regina's will: 'The rich woman had willed the house with all its contents, the whole estate, almost her entire fortune, to the chauffeur. To her husband she left only a meagre life interest, a pittance; and some objects without any special value, as keepsakes.' It was under one of these 'keepsakes', a grotesquely tasteless portrait of the model for Regina, that Anna Kavan wrote this impotent act of revenge against her dead mother. The portrait was to remain in place watching over Anna for the rest of her life as a writer.

Forgotten in the literary world, Anna was forced to publish the book with a 'vanity press', paying £50 for the privilege. Some curse must have hung over the enterprise, for no sooner had review copies been sent out than Downie went bankrupt and was unable to distribute the book. Reviews were generally good; Edwin Muir, a consistent admirer, praised the book in *The Sunday Times*, but eventually almost the entire edition was pulped. An uncredited newspaper clipping among Anna Kavan's papers recounts:

> Authoress in a most unusual plight is Miss Anna
> Kavan. Her novel *A Scarcity of Love* was given high
> praise by reviewers; a big public demand followed. But
> only 500 copies are available for distribution. Mr
> Oliver Moxon, a fellow author, and managing director
> of a book distributing firm, tells me the situation has
> arisen because of difficulties encountered by the
> publisher after review copies had been sent out. 'My
> heart bleeds for Miss Kavan,' he said. 'It is her first
> book for eight years, and, like her last, *Sleep Has His
> House*, deals with the tragedy of a woman of abnormal
> mentality.' Now Mr Moxon is trying to arrange a
> second printing.

There was no second printing in Anna's lifetime. It must have been galling to her to have to part-pay for publication, but the fact that it all came to nothing must have been doubly frustrating.

It was at this nadir of her career as a writer that Anna Kavan met Peter Owen, who was to be her chief publisher for the rest of her career. Owen recalls that they were introduced by Diana Johns, a bookseller whom Rhys Davies had introduced to Anna and whose shop she frequented. At a subsequent meeting Anna gave Peter Owen the manuscript of a novel, *Eagles' Nest*, which he published in 1957. Kavan was then living in 99 Peel Street, a house she had converted, not without difficulty, into flats. Following the depressing pattern of her life at this time, she had quarrelled with Herman Schrijver, having originally agreed to let one of the flats to Charles Burkhart, then having withdrawn the offer. The builders' work had been slipshod and she was taking them to court. Though her relationship with Peter Owen was to be occasionally stormy, it was his belief in her as a writer, coupled with a refusal to let her publish work that he considered substandard, which kept Anna writing and publishing through the ensuing decade of generally admiring reviews but restricted sales.

Eagles' Nest was Kavan's most directly Kafkaesque fiction; the story of an anonymous male hero and his unequal battle with a malevolent, sinisterly hostile world. He begins by working as an 'advertising artist' in a department store, 'the most degrading of the whole succession of haphazard make-shift jobs which had replaced the absorbing, congenial work for which I had been trained'. To escape, he accepts the offer of a job as library assistant to 'the Administrator' of a large distant estate. The estate, set in a tropical landscape, some-times verdant and lush, sometimes arid, is clearly based on Tevis's house in Monterey. *Eagles' Nest* is, like Kafka's *The Castle*, firmly set in a nightmarish country of the imagination, described by Anna Kavan in one of the memorable delinea-tions of an internal/external landscape that she was later to evoke to perfection in *Ice*:

> I felt I could have put out my hand and touched the
> volcanic hills, rising like islands from this unstable
> brilliance, mirages floating in the transparent dazzle.
> Beyond them, nothing was to be seen but mountains,
> all of the same stark, forbidding outline, flat-topped,
> rectilinear, savagely coloured and depthless-looking, as
> if painted on the cobalt sky; crowding one behind
> another like a gigantic city of vast skyscrapers, or a
> monstrous cemetery of colossal coffins stood up on end.
> There was something frighteningly strange about these
> angular identical mountains, so different from the
> grandeur of the snow-capped mountains I knew, and
> seeming to have no life or soul, as they stretched away
> to infinity, range beyond range, gruesome in their
> impressiveness, overpowering, a horror of dead rock.

It is soon evident that life for the hero at Eagles' Nest will be little different from the life he has left; a series of unending, petty humiliations. The Administrator is absent and he is dealt with by a series of functionaries and servants who subtly endeavour to convince him of his own powerlessness. As she had once described Monterey with its panoplies of footmen and butlers, Anna Kavan describes the 'extraordinary system' governing Eagles' Nest as 'something huge, nebulous and vaguely python-like, enveloping the place in its folds, crushing out all happiness and spontaneous life'. Everyone spies on everyone else, for unexplained reasons. 'You don't understand our ways,' the hero is told, '. . . which aren't as simple as they appear.' Sometimes the book operates on the level of dream, lapsing occasionally into hallucination, but the hero never understands the underlying situation. Eventually he meets the Administrator, who tells him that, because of his past actions, there is no job for him:

'People don't understand Eagles' Nest because, to us, everything is a symbol of something else, and every sign can be interpreted in various ways. . . .
Signs wrongly read, wrongly combined or chosen, can result only in false conclusions, and judgments that are unreliable. All I ask of you is not to judge me more harshly than our own code, which makes allowances for human limitations, and doesn't expect the impossible – not even of its administrator.'

The hero is expelled for having transgressed some law which he does not understand. He refuses the helping hand of the Administrator:

Wherever I looked, I encountered the same blank rejection, as though, by rejecting the hand, I had initiated a mass-reaction in my surroundings. With

dreadful finality, the room itself was casting me into
outer darkness. I was already demoralised; and now,
faced with the chill indifference of everything around
me, I grew panic-stricken. I felt the panic of a solitary
benighted traveller, whose guide has vanished, taking
with him the only light, as, wrenching the door open
blindly, in mindless terror, I stumbled out of the room.

This maze of a novel, which wanders between dream
imagery, the 'second secret life' of the narrator, and objective
description, puzzled most critics: oddly its most sympathetic
notice was in *The Lady*, not an organ noted for avant-garde
sympathies. It took nearly twenty years to sell the first edition
of the novel and, when it was republished in 1976, even as
sympathetic a reviewer as Duncan Fallowell, writing in *The
Spectator*, was mystified. Though he thought Kavan 'the best
English woman writer since Virginia Woolf', the deliberately
enigmatic nature of the book perplexed him. 'An
extraordinary degree of suspense is achieved by imperceptible
undertones never thrown away. Every sentence contains a
mystery and as these accumulate so does the longing for at
least one clear explanation.'

The book might be subject to a variety of explanations. The
hero is, like Anna Kavan, an artist, out of place in the *haute-
bourgeois* atmosphere of Eagles' Nest and ignorant of, or
unwilling to conform with, its unwritten codes. The house is
described as a 'museum' (as Kavan had once described
Monterey) and on one level the book can be read as an
imaginative recasting of her experiences in South Africa. In
many ways its hero is reminiscent of Swithin Chance, the
'accidental man' who was the hero of Helen Ferguson's last
novel, and perhaps the gap between Helen Ferguson and
Anna Kavan was not so great as the radical method of *Asylum
Piece* would suggest. In many ways *Eagles' Nest* is a quite
conventional novel, and an attempt to bend her talent to a

more orthodox form of expression was to be characteristic of all of Anna's fiction throughout the fifties. It was her response to the generally anti-experimental mood prevailing in British culture for most of that decade. If poetry can be taken as the most sensitive barometer of this trend, the New Romantics and Apocalyptics of the forties had withered, to be replaced by 'The Movement', a grouping consisting primarily of dons who wrote verse of calculated formality, clarity and high cerebral content. The main trend in the British novel of the fifties was the emergence of a lower middle class, vaguely malcontented university-educated hero, dubbed, in a rather exaggerated way 'the Angry Young Man'. The source of his discontent was sociological rather than psychological, however: it was as if the experimentalism of the forties had never existed.

In 1958 Kavan followed *Eagles' Nest* with a book of short stories, *A Bright Green Field*. In many ways the most characteristic of Anna Kavan's books, it explores all of her previous, and forthcoming, literary preoccupations. Stories such as 'Annunciation', 'Mouse, Shoes' and 'New and Splendid' explore the world of the threatened or oppressed child. Some stories are clealy set in locations drawn from her travels: 'One of the Hot Spots', 'The End of Something' and 'Lonely Unholy Shore' drawing from her time in the South Pacific, and 'Ice Storm' located in New York and Connecticut. They range in manner from the near-realism of 'Annunciation', a superb evocation of a young girl's fear at her first menstruation, to the surreal free association of 'All Saints'. In the final story of the book, a sixty-page novella entitled 'New and Splendid', she moves towards the genre which has gained the unfortunate appellation of science fiction. The story has the familiar Kavan hero, a frightened, orphaned child, in this case a boy, going to meet an uncle in a city which is an imaginative reworking of New York, divided between the High City of luxury and the Lanes of squalor. Again following

a familiar pattern, he is first accepted then cast out, conde-
mned to live in the Lanes for no reason he can discover.
Images from the chill, lonely childhood of Helen Woods rise
throughout the book, as in this passage from 'Christmas
Wishes'

> Precisely as if I were inside the thermometer, the
> sinking mercury drags me down a few years in the
> wrong direction. It's hopeless, evidently; I'll never get
> back to the place where I want to be. Instead now, the
> whole taste of my childhood comes up like vomit. Like
> a timid stray animal, small and frightened and on my
> guard, I'm walking on tiptoe through a palatial great
> house that seems completely deserted. The silence is
> terrifying. Not a sound, not a soul, anywhere.
> Overhead, the chandeliers spout their petrified jets and
> fountains in diamond rivers of arctic light. I peep into
> a vast empty room, splendidly furnished, where a
> Christmas tree is towering up to the ceiling, sparkling
> with toys and trinkets, with wondrous decorations, gold
> and silver fish, delicate little iridescent birds with
> transparent tremulous tails, jewel-bright orbs of every
> colour, strands of shimmering tinsel, delicious bonbons
> and crystallized fruits, all lit up by countless electric
> candles. What a strange lonely brilliance blazes from
> this tree, all alone in its splendour, in the magnificent
> room! With what a chill unblinking unfestive dazzle
> the candles shine! Obviously this is no place for me,
> this aloof grand celebration on which I've intruded;
> from which, insignificantly, I retire in apologetic haste,
> hurrying off, my arms clutching my chest to quiet my
> clamorous heartbeats.

Though sales of both books were low, Kavan had made a
return after the publishing débâcle of *A Scarcity of Love*. She

had pulled back again from the brink of literary extinction as, Lazarus-like, she had done from personal extinction. As the fifties progressed, she had some cause to be optimistic.

13

The Man Who Never Paid

*

Literary activities apart, the mid-fifties were busy years for Anna Kavan. There were to be no more travels, as these excursions usually required a period of detoxification, and there were no more spells in sanatoriums or nursing homes. Secure as Anna was with a regular supply of legal heroin from Dr Bluth, her life became increasingly hermetic; a characteristic she was to express architecturally in the house she designed and built at 19 Hillsleigh Road. 'Like a Chinese puzzle-box,' one friend described it, and its complex interlocking rooms and densely foliated garden were increasingly to become part of the mechanism by which she kept the world at bay.

The house was divided into two flats, Anna occupying the upper floor and the downstairs flat being let. An article by Edna McKenna entitled 'A Spot of High Class Mindbending Needs an L Shaped Room' described the flat to readers of the 'Homestyle' pages of a London newspaper. 'Most flats waste a terrible amount of space with rooms opening off corridors, and doors everywhere. I wanted something that would be very easy to run, so that I could get on with my writing,' Anna is quoted as saying. 'All the walls in the flat are white to add a feeling of spaciousness, and the polished parquet floors have off-white Indian rugs.' It was as compact as a ship's cabin, the author of the article commented, noticing also that her décor was a fine blend of the antique and the exotic. From her Burmese days, a Burmese gong, which served as a coffee-table, and a figurine of Ranga, the child-stealing witch of

Burmese mythology, were prominent, as were her mother's harp and portrait. The plan of the flat consisted of a single L-shaped room which divided the living and dining space from the kitchen and bedroom. Close to the latter was the bathroom. Outside was a small, high-walled garden which Kavan tended daily, lush and overgrown as a painting by Rousseau. The blinds were often drawn, the rooms overheated. The high garden walls were the cause of a lawsuit brought by Anna's neighbours, who objected to them: the electric underfloor heating, a relative novelty in fifties' London, was unfortunately laid upside-down by the builders, thus propelling its heat into the downstairs flat.

Anna developed a reputation for being unable to get on with women; one which seems to be borne out in the pattern of her friendships. She never broke with her childhood friend of Malvern College days, Ann Ledbrook, and in due course her daughter Rose Knox-Peebles was to become a friend also. Recalling Hillsleigh Road, she writes:

> Her furniture was a mixture of old and new (G-plan?); a dressing table with the top drawer filled with make-up and instructions for making up eyes cut out from a magazine and stuck to the bottom of the drawer. Two big circular mirrors on stalks stood on top of it (not well described but, at the time, it seemed like a very advanced design). There was a lounging chair that I think was covered in artificial leopard skin. It sounds revolting but it suited her. Always white or off-white upholstery and carpets. Her bed had a canopy over it. Her use of space was ingenious: the house was like a three-dimensional jigsaw puzzle. I was always fascinated by the amount of room she had, and how it fitted in. There were masses of books, paintings and objects about. She lived at the top, reached by an outside staircase. At the back was a garden, all green

like a jungle, thick and mysterious, and the ground, I seem to remember, had been covered with pebbles. It was the kind of garden that had no flower beds.

Anna was fortunate in having the wherewithal and talent to construct such a highly personalized environment in which to spend the rest of her days. In her initial choice of downstairs tenant she was less fortunate.

Gerald Hamilton, if his stories are to be believed, had known almost every charlatan in modern European history from Rasputin onward, and had been decorated by almost every obscure or extinct European power for equally obscure 'services rendered'. He had been in Berlin in the decadent twenties and had served as model for the masochistic 'fixer' in Christopher Isherwood's *Mr Norris Changes Trains*. A raconteur, epicure and inveterate snob, aged seventy and with no visible means of support, he was dying as he had always lived – beyond his means and one step ahead of the writ-servers. He had been one of Anna's neighbours in Peel Street, and they had a mutual friend in Peter Watson, the aesthete who had financed *Horizon*, and later the Institute of Contemporary Arts. Despite his political opinions, now rabidly right wing, and a reputation for financial misdealing which must have reached her ears, Anna chose him as her lodger and they both moved into the house in June 1958, 'the cement hardly dry'.

Barely a month had passed before Anna gave him notice to quit after he complained about the noise coming from her flat. Nevertheless, he remained there until 11th November, during which time he paid no rent, then decamped to the Canary Isles. For Anna at least, he seems to have had some charm, for she forgave him to the extent of inviting him for dinner, then presenting him with a writ of her own. Some found him sinister: to Julian Maclaren-Ross he was 'like Aleister Crowley, a dangerous man. I'd call him the last of the dangerous men'. To Anna the only threat he posed was financial, and his 'danger' lay in the demi-world of young toughs whom he favoured sexually and, like Crowley, in his completely unremorseful attitude to his own vices and failings. Told that Sartre had dubbed Genet a saint, Hamilton commented that he would probably think he, Gerald Hamilton, was an archangel. Writs continued to flow from Anna, who was owed exactly £100, for at least a year, until she gave up the effort. Despite it all she remained friendly with Gerald Hamilton, who admired her work and gave her, in partial recompense, a Chinese shawl. She even had a grudging admiration for his method. 'You simply can't treat people as human beings,' she once wrote to Raymond Marriott in a fit of annoyance, 'they only despise you for it and take advantage. Treat them rough like Gerald does, and they'll eat out of your hand.'

The flat was briefly occupied by Janice Picton (about whom more later), but early in 1960 the tenancy of the lower flat was taken over by Raymond Marriott. He was to be Anna's lodger, friend and confidant for the rest of her life.

14

Who Are You?

*

As the sixties dawned, the pattern of life for Anna Kavan in her remaining years was set. She still dabbled in house renovation and would occasionally accompany friends to the theatre, but more and more her life turned inward, to her writing, her garden and her 'Chinese puzzle-box' flat. In spite of his living downstairs, she wrote quite frequently to Raymond Marriott, commenting early in 1960 that she was 'in a terrible situation, financially'.

The true nature of her finances was a mystery to those who knew Anna. She often pleaded poverty while admitting that the standard of living in which she had been reared meant that her definition of the term was different from that of her friends, most of whom were considerably poorer than she. In the fifties she had published two books, for which she had received advances of £25 each from Peter Owen. Neither had earned her any royalties and these sums, plus payment for a few stories published in magazines, meant that her total literary income was under £100. On her mother's death, she had received £6,000 from the sale of the Manor House at Earley. This had been invested and gave her a taxable annual income of £350. It would seem that the £600 a year allowance continued to be paid by Hugh Tevis, though it was made clear that this was a 'grace and favour' payment and not hers by legal right.

In 1958, after leaving Dr Bluth's house in Campden Street, she was knocked down by a car. Her injuries were not very serious, but she was immobilized for some time and developed an ulcer on her foot. In claiming compensation for loss of earnings, she declared that a house she had bought for £4,250 in October 1959 had been improved at a cost of £2,000 and was about to be sold for £8,000. If one assumes a similar profit margin on all of her transactions, it becomes clear that most of her income in the fifties derived from property development. This line of activity lessened in the sixties, and penury may have been a contributory cause to her increasing reclusiveness. She continued to write and to submit work to Peter Owen but none of it, for one reason or another, was suitable for publication. Around 1960 she submitted a novel which Owen rejected as being 'too short'. Later, when his firm had achieved more financial stability, he asked to see it again, only to be told that it had been destroyed. The battle against ill-health and depression continued, fits of the latter usually manifesting themselves in the conviction that she had, somehow, been cursed from birth. 'Why do I *always* have such fiendish bad luck? Even over things where nobody *could* go wrong. It never seems my fault but I suppose it must be an obscure manifestation of the Death Wish or something,' she complained to Raymond Marriott in June 1962.

For the first time in a number of years she had written a book, a novella, with which she was pleased. Composed during 1961 and submitted to Peter Owen early in 1962, *Who Are You?* was a fictional reworking of the collapse of her first marriage, which had already been fictionalized in the Helen Ferguson novel, *Let Me Alone*. However, *Who Are You?* is a far darker and more experimental reading of these events, and has a curious alternative ending which puzzled many reviewers. Anna Kavan explained:

The people in the story live through the same situation twice over. But they are not the same, and the outcome is different, because the element of nightmare which

predominates in the first experience is in abeyance
later. Their identities are equally real or unreal in both
cases. The 'you' of the bird's question could be either,
or both of them – or neither.

. . . I wanted to abandon realistic writing insofar as
it describes exclusively events in the physical
environment, and to make the reader aware of the
existence of the different, though just as real, 'reality'
which lies just beyond the surface of ordinary daily life
and the surface aspect of things. I am convinced that a
vast, exciting new territory is waiting to be explored by
the writer in that direction.

To explore it, unconventional techniques are
required. For instance, the repetition of certain
incidents in the same or slightly differing forms is
meant to create a three-dimensional effect – an effect
in depth – and to show that there is no 'absolute'
reality, but that every happening will appear different
at different times to different people.

By avoiding any detailed characterisation or plot, I
wanted to free the reader from the actual written word,
so that he would not be trapped in a piece of
reportage, but stimulated to relate what is written to
his own and the whole human condition, which of
course is again different for each individual.

Peter Owen thought the book was too short to stand on its
own but was willing to consider it with a selection of short
stories. Yet he was pessimistic about the sales potential for
short stories, a form that has seldom found favour with the
British book-buying public, and urged her to work on a
full-length novel. Eventually the book was taken up by Scorpion Press, a small publishing house based in Lowestoft,
Suffolk, which published it to general acclaim in 1963. There
was talk that the firm might reissue *A Scarcity of Love*, but

relations between Anna and her new publisher soon soured. Writing to Raymond Marriott, who was seeking a publisher for his poetry, she commented in March 1963: 'I see my publisher does poetry, but I wouldn't recommend him to my worst enemy.'

Who Are You? was appreciated both by reviewers and the general reading public. Jean Rhys, writing to her friend Francis Wyndham on madness in literature, specifically as it related to her novel *Wide Sargasso Sea*, was moved to comment:

> I've never read a long novel about a mad mind or an unusual mind or anybody's mind at all. Yet it is the only thing that matters and so difficult to put over without being dull.
>
> Anna Kavan's stories I like, and I have her novel *Who Are You?* Very short, but what a splendid title. If only I'd thought of it – but it would have been too late in any case. . . .

Though the two women never met, the admiration was mutual, Rose Knox-Peebles recalling that 'Anna introduced me to Jean Rhys for which I am eternally grateful'.

A more public admirer was the American novelist, critic and diarist, Anaïs Nin, whose enthusiasm dated back to the years of *Asylum Piece* and *The House of Sleep*. Both women had a common English publisher in Peter Owen and, in the late fifties, Nin had written an admiring letter to Anna Kavan to which she eventually responded after a lapse of four years. Following the publication of *Who Are You?*, Nin wrote again: 'I asked Peter Owen about you, but as you know better than anyone else, people can only *see* what is like them. In spite of his respect and admiration, he could give me no image of you. . . . Who are you, Anna Kavan?' On 18th July 1963 Anna wrote with an air of weariness to Raymond Marriott: 'I shall *have* to answer Anaïs Nin now.' She never did. Nor, despite the fact that Nin's subjective explorations were close to her own territory, did she ever express any enthusiasm for Nin's work.

Anna's personal literary enthusiasms were limited and almost exclusively male, though she had a great liking for Djuna Barnes's *Nightwood* and the work of Nadine Gordimer. She developed a reputation for disliking women, especially if they were writers. After the departure of Gerald Hamilton, Peter Owen had suggested at a dinner party that she let the downstairs flat to Janice Picton, who was then working for him. The suggestion was coolly received and, when Anna left the room, Rhys Davies leaned over and whispered to Owen: 'Don't. She hates women.' Miss Picton's later tenancy proved extremely brief. The novelist Olivia Manning, a friend of both Rhys Davies and Herman Schrijver, was invited to a dinner party during which Anna refused to talk, then pointedly started reading magazines.

Writers she admired included, surprisingly, Anthony Powell, and less surprisingly, Julien Green. She was very keen on Robbe-Grillet and other practitioners of the *nouveau roman*, though not, predictably, Nathalie Sarraute. Though she delighted in his company, Rhys Davies felt that privately she had little enthusiasm for his writing. Her closest woman friend was Rose Knox-Peebles, who was some years younger than Anna, not a writer, and who regarded her with some awe. Rose was a close neighbour in Kensington and, as Anna's health deteriorated and crises became more frequent, she became drawn into the elaborate support system to which all Anna's friends belonged. As the only driver among them, Rose's role was frequently that of chauffeur. She remembers:

> She was impractical, but I don't know if she really couldn't do practical things with her hands, or whether it was a feminine wile that she had always practised to

get things done for her. Anyway, by the time I was
seeing quite a lot of her, I think it was genuine. She
couldn't change her typewriter ribbon, so I would do
this for her – and I believe the man who delivered her
bread from Barkers would change lightbulbs for her.
She was liked by tradesmen etc., certainly she had a
very good relationship with her cleaning woman, who
was motherly towards her – I think she liked being
with people who treated her as if she were an
'everyday' sort of person. . . .

She had a thing about clothes. I first remember her
as someone who would send my mother boxes of
clothes to see if she would like them. They always
smelt of her scent (Trésor, by Lancôme). . . . From
time to time my mother would go up to London and
she would meet Anna and take me with her. I was very
shy, and I knew Anna was a writer and an intellectual
but she was always sweet to me and, if I could, I would
talk to her about books. Later I always passed on my
Times Literary Supplements. . . .

Anna was very beautiful, not conventionally but in
the overall effect. She had a husky voice and spoke in
a very slow drawl, as if through cigarette smoke. She
was rather like some of those bleached forties' heroines
who smoked cynically through long cigarette holders.
Her eyes were strange and seemed not to focus when
she spoke, and of course she had pin-prick pupils. I
always knew that she took drugs: my mother never
concealed it but spoke about it matter-of-factly. I think
one problem now is that the kind of media attention
paid to drugs would make them far more important in
some respects in Anna's life than, in fact, they were.
The habit was a part of her. She seemed to have tamed
it, or at least, organised it. It was like being a diabetic;
a question of having regularly to inject a substance

which is necessary to you. Her hair was white, like
those film stars I mention above, not 'elderly' white at
all. She was very thin, wore slacks and loose jumpers,
flat shoes, pale pink lipstick and had eyebrows that
looked as artificial as Marlene Dietrich's. . . .

Anna once told me that she had so many clothes
because she was so frightened of the saleswomen who
were in shops in those days that she never dared walk
out of a shop without buying anything. At any rate,
often she never wore these clothes, and I imagine she
also bought clothes as a comfort: if you are unhappy,
the best therapy is to go out and buy a dress.

Such happiness and satisfaction as may have come from the
favourable reception of *Who Are You?* was to be short-lived.
On 4th October 1963 Anna wrote that Dr Bluth was being
hospitalized owing to a recurrence of the heart problem that
had plagued him for many years. By now the patient/doctor
relationship was blurred to the extent that he was as dependent on her as she was on him.

15

Waiting for Death

*

In March of the following year, after being discharged from hospital, Dr Bluth died suddenly of a heart attack at home, before the ambulance which his wife had summoned arrived. After the initial shock of his death had subsided, Anna composed a brief obituary for *The Times*, and laid plans for her personal response:

> The death in London last week of Dr Karl Theodore Bluth, the poet, playwright and essayist, should not pass unnoticed. Dr Bluth, whose anti-fascist views forced him to leave Germany in 1934, was principally known in this country as a medical consultant and a psychiatrist, though among his publications in England are two long essays in the periodical *Horizon*, 'The Revival of Schelling' and 'Swiss Humanism', and a book, *Leibnitz the European*, published by Drummond. Many British poets and painters were his patients as well as other refugees, all of whom found him an unfailing source of stimulation and encouragement.

She begged Raymond Marriott to keep her company. 'Will you anyhow spend as many evenings with me as you can endure? I will do my best to behave normally,' she wrote. In fact she had come to the conclusion that life without Bluth was intolerable. In the twenty years since they had met he, and the heroin he had prescribed, had kept at bay the 'obsessional suicide' syndrome he had diagnosed. According to Raymond Marriott, there had been a pact between them that their deaths should coincide. Anna consulted a solicitor and, on 13th April, drew up a will dividing the bulk of her estate between Raymond Marriott and Rhys Davies. She bequeathed £500 to Charlotte Cousins, her cleaning lady, and another £500 to Mrs Theophila Bluth, as some recompense for the anguish she had caused her over the years. Having settled her worldly affairs, Anna Kavan took an exceptionally large dosage of heroin and went to bed.

Raymond Marriott and Rhys Davies had been prepared for this eventuality. Anna had been so distraught that she had come to regard Dr Bluth's death as an act of betrayal, of 'selling her down the river', as she put it. Both men broke into her flat and had her rushed to hospital, where her life was saved, much to her initial annoyance:

> I was desperate, determined not to go on living. In
> front of those who were left, I put on an act and
> concealed my intention. But, accidentally, or thinking
> one of my so-called friends really was well-disposed
> towards me, I must have given some indication of what
> I meant to do. So these people frustrated me, forced
> me to live my impossible life and go on suffering. I
> can't say how profoundly I resent their interference. I
> write this to prevent any misunderstanding.

Most people who knew Anna Kavan in her later years comment on her frequently wilful and antisocial behaviour. Much of it is attributable to the years remaining after Dr Bluth's death, when she increasingly turned to heroin as a palliative and withdrew even further from normal human intercourse. After Dr Bluth died, she told Peter Owen, she herself was only 'waiting for death'.

Partly as therapy she began to write a series of stories dedicated to Dr Bluth, several of which were published in *Julia and the Bazooka*. By October 1965 they were nearly completed, and she sent some to her friend, Herman Schrijver:

> I promised to write something about K.T., and each
> of these separate pieces is about him. Some are written
> 'straight', others, rather more fantastic, are in the first
> person, sometimes as if he were the writer, sometimes
> as if I was.
> As a whole it's meant to be a sort of love story – a
> lament for a death – and therefore I feel it ought to be
> published before the other MS read by Francis King.
> I'm not sure that the order of the pieces is right; and
> there are one or two more not quite finished.

Four of the stories in the posthumous volume *Julia and the Bazooka* deal directly with Dr Bluth: 'The Mercedes', 'The Zebra-Struck', 'A Town Garden' and 'Obsessional'. He is the 'M' of whom she wrote: 'All these years he'd been saying we'd drive off together. I simply couldn't believe he would go without me.' Her obsessive devotion to Dr Bluth is best expressed in 'The Zebra-Struck':

> Their relationship had not been clearly defined. It had
> seemed to achieve itself spontaneously, without effort
> on either side, and with no preliminary doubts or
> misunderstandings. To her it was both inevitable and
> invested with dreamlike wonder that, among all the
> earth's teeming millions, she should have met the one
> being complementary to herself. It was as if she'd
> always been lost and living in chaos, until this man
> had appeared like a magician and put everything right.
> The few brief flashes of happiness she had known
> before had always been against a permanent
> background of black isolation, a terrifying utter

loneliness, the metaphysical horror of which she'd
never been able to convey to any lover or psychiatrist.
Now suddenly, miraculously, that terror had gone; she
was no longer alone, and could only respond with
boundless devotion to the miracle worker.

He was twelve years older than she and looked older,
and as she looked less than her age, they were
sometimes taken, much to his amusement, for father
and daughter. Her own father had died while she was
a child, she couldn't remember him, and she had
perhaps always been looking for a substitute father.
Well-suited to this role, the man seemed appropriately
her superior, with his benevolence, knowledge and
academic degrees; his reputation, his poetry, his
experience of the world; his successes, catastrophes and
adventures. He was often very gay, and often indulged
in fantastic imaginings; but also he often seemed to be
evolving strange and significant thoughts behind his
vast forehead.

Apart from his role as her soul-mate, Dr Bluth had been for
more than twenty years the source of her legally prescribed
heroin. 'After his death, a search for another doctor was one of
her bitter pilgrimages,' Rhys Davies writes. And, apart from
his death, there were further complications arising from
changed official attitudes towards drug-taking.

The pattern of heroin use had substantially altered during
the fifties, with a decline in the numbers who had acquired the
habit as a result of medical treatment and an increase in
recreational users who had become addicted. In 1961 an
interdepartmental committee, the Brain Committee, was set
up to review drug policy in the light of this changing pattern.
The problem was still so numerically small that the Committee was unable to suggest any changes to current practices.
However, in the early sixties there was another sharp increase

in the incidence of addiction, and in 1964 the Committee was reconvened.

Its report in 1965 noted the increase in the number of addicts and linked this to overprescription by a number of doctors in London. Surplus drugs were then being sold by addicts to a growing black market. The Committee suggested a number of controls limiting the number of doctors authorized to prescribe heroin which, in effect, meant attendance by addicts at out-patient clinics. They also proposed that there be compulsory powers to detain and treat addicts.

The latter recommendation was not accepted by the government, but the fear of compulsory detoxification grew to loom large in Anna Kavan's mind and she furiously stockpiled drugs in case that proposal became a legal eventuality. All the other recommendations of the Committee became law. Legislation was passed enabling regulations to be made requiring the compulsory notification of addicts, and restricting the supply of heroin or cocaine to addicts for the purpose of treating their addiction. Licences to prescribe these drugs to treat addiction were then granted only to doctors working in hospitals or similar institutions, with the result that the treatment of addicts was removed from general practitioners to the hospital service. Special treatment centres were set up in several National Health Service hospitals under the clinical direction of consultant psychiatrists.

It was not until the final years of her life that Anna Kavan was forced to attend such a clinic on a regular basis. Despite government efforts, 'junkie doctors', often operating privately, continued throughout the sixties to cater for a growing addict population. Though she never found a doctor as sympathetic as Dr Bluth, Anna managed to obtain a constant supply of heroin in quantities more than sufficient to maintain her habit.

That the sixties were to be a decade more attuned to Anna Kavan's literary sensibility than the fifties had been became apparent as the era unfolded. On 8th June 1964 she attended the first London 'Happening', and later wrote about it with great enthusiasm to Raymond Marriott:

> I understand that a Happening is defined as a 'planned extension of the environment, which surrounds the audience or visitor and may consist of absolutely anything', so it is obvious the unfamiliar terms are easily ridiculed or made to sound pretentious. But if both the Happening and the Environment are to be taken as signs of a general revolt against realism in the imaginative arts, why has the Happening of June 8th been considered as too insignificant even to be mentioned by critics of books and plays?
>
> I would have thought it would have been of special importance to playwrights and novelists now that the documentary has practically abolished all other forms, and threatens the very existence of creativity. Reportage inevitably becomes universal when all facts are instantaneously made available to everyone everywhere; the fragile living impulse of imagination could easily be swamped and extinguished altogether by the flood of information pouring in all the time from all sides.

If these ideas have a slight ring of familiarity, it is probably because Rhys Davies was currently reading that seminal book of sixties prophecy, Marshall McLuhan's *Understanding Media*, and had doubtless discussed its implications with Anna Kavan.

The emerging culture of the sixties fascinated Anna. In many ways she was a most atypical addict, since none of her circle were themselves addicts and, thanks to the ministrations of Dr Bluth, she had been protected from the squalor and uncertainty of the black market. Heroin addiction as a literary theme began to emerge in the late fifties and early sixties, notably in the work of William Burroughs and Alex Trocchi, but Anna showed no recorded interest in their books which dealt, by and large, with an underground milieu alien to her rather protected circumstances.

Changes in drug legislation and the need to attend clinics led her to come into contact with the new drug subculture, which she embraced with some enthusiasm. She was already familiar with marijuana, having smoked it in New York in the company of Charles Fuller and his friends. Apparently she reacquainted herself with the drug, then gaining great popularity and almost sacramental status, commenting in a note to Raymond Marriott: 'I listened for sixty minutes to a talk on marijuana (what they call Mary Venna). What incredible rubbish is talked. Really, this drug business is beyond belief.' And, as is evidenced by some typically vague psychedelic meanderings, she used LSD on at least one occasion with apparently pleasurable results. That this experiment, with a drug capable of triggering attacks in both actual and latent schizophrenics, was successful, is further evidence that, whatever label may be attached to her mental condition, she was unlikely to have been clinically schizophrenic. It was a dangerous drug for a depressive to take, but the experience was enjoyable. LSD colours some of the stories posthumously collected by Rhys Davies in *My Soul in China*. And, at this time when psychedelic clubs like Middle Earth and the Roundhouse flourished, Rhys Davies records that 'she asked to be taken to a typical "pop" den in the West End, where hippies danced and sat about in their plenitude of hair and their glowering and glamour and blankness. Such stories as "Tiny Thing" and one or two others were the result'. Rhys Davies also says that she was a frequent user of amphetamine, a drug commonly available during the fifties which developed a large underground market in the sixties. If the drug subculture was a source of fascination to her, she remained somewhat puzzled by its argot. 'What', she asked

Raymond Marriott [himself hardly likely to know] 'does it mean to say something is a gas?'

Other elements of the sixties' upheaval were less welcome. The BBC launched itself into what was, at the time, a daring venture into current socio-political satire in a late-night programme called *That Was the Week That Was*. It was not to Anna Kavan's taste. 'TWTWTW surpassed itself in boring vulgarity last night', she recorded primly on one occasion. However, both she and Raymond Marriott became fans of an idiosyncratic children's programme of a science-fiction bent which had just begun its long run: *Dr Who*.

If Anna Kavan had ever been marginally a political creature, her interest had now lapsed. In response to a questionnaire circulated by Cecil Woolf to a number of writers, she wrote irritably to Raymond Marriott: '"Would you like to express your views on the U.S. intervention in Vietnam? How should the conflict be resolved?" I can't think of anything I could usefully say. I don't understand a thing anyhow.' And in a further note: 'You're right about ballsup of civilisation – I keep saying *I don't give a damn what happens once I'm dead*. Why should I? It's nothing to do with me.' Despite this streak of nihilism, she remained a regular subscriber to the left-wing *New Statesman*.

All the while Anna struggled to write, to paint and to conquer the despair she felt. In late 1966 there was a lapse, when she deliberately overdosed, then panicked and called Rhys Davies to tell him what she had done. He and Raymond Marriott broke into her flat and, once more, she was rushed to hospital and saved.

In response to Peter Owen's suggestion that she work on a novel rather than short stories, Anna had been working for some years on a new book. It was a dreamlike transmogrification of her wanderings during the Second World War, part *nouveau roman* and part (though she hardly knew it) science fiction. Early in 1966 she submitted a draft of *The Cold World* to Owen for comment.

16

The Cold World into Ice

*

The book provisionally titled *The Cold World* had 'kicked around for quite some time', in the words of its publisher, Peter Owen. A very early draft had been completed at the time of Dr Bluth's death in March 1964. In late 1965, another version was submitted to Weidenfeld and Nicolson by Francis King, who was then working for them as a literary adviser. Though he recommended the book for publication, it was eventually rejected. 'There was some agonized discussion as to whether Anna Kavan would actually *sell*,' he recalls. On 23rd March 1966 Peter Owen gave it a highly qualified acceptance:

> I am sorry to be rather negative again. I thought it might help you to have a sight of a reader's report from someone who knows your work and is keen on it. We feel that the material would have been better as a story rather than a novel as it seems to be very much on one level. One of the criticisms is that the characters do not really come to life. If you were interested to do some revision, we could make some suggestions. In that case, would you let me know, and I am holding the manuscript meanwhile for this reason. Although I would reconsider the book if revisions were made I couldn't, at this stage, definitely promise to publish it depending on how any revisions work out. I do think that there now seems to be an upsurge of interest in your work; it is important that nothing but the best should appear.

Anna replied on the following day:

Many thanks for your letter and for letting me see
the reader's report. It's hard for me to say anything
about revising without knowing at all the extent or
nature of the revision you have in mind. If you would
care to give me a rough idea of this I would be able to
tell you whether I see any hope of a result that would
satisfy both of us.

How interesting that your reader finds the writing a
mixture of Kafka and the Avengers – this expresses
quite accurately the effect I was aiming at. Considering
Kafka's reputation and the success of The Avengers, I
can't think why you don't want the book as it is!

On 29th March Anna wrote saying that she had rewritten
parts of the book and mounted a more detailed defence of her
current work:

I appreciate your only wanting to print my best work,
but you always make comparisons with something I
wrote in the past, as if there was an absolute standard
of good writing which didn't change. Even if this is so,
I can't keep on all my life writing in the same way.
Unless I feel a compulsion to write a book in a certain
way before I start, I know it won't be any good, so I
can only write as I want to. *A Scarcity of Love* was
what I wanted to write, and the best writing I could do
at that time. The world is now quite different and so is
my life in it. One reacts to the environment and
atmosphere one lives in, one absorbs outside influences,
and my writing changes with the conditions outside.
This kind of adventure story seems to be in the air just
now, which is probably why I wanted to write a book
of that sort in my own language and with my own

symbolism. It is not meant to be realistic writing. It's a sort of present day fable, in which detailed characterisation would be out of place.

On 6th April Anna wrote requesting that the manuscript be returned. This letter crossed with a parcel containing the manuscript and a letter from Philip Inman, Peter Owen's reader and editor. He said that he did not expect all her writing to be like that in *A Scarcity of Love*, but felt that all Anna Kavan's work should be as satisfactory in its own terms as that book had been. He felt that the character of the girl was too vague to sustain interest and that the narrator's wanderings were too pointless, ending:

I know I am open to the charge of misunderstanding
the dreamlike nature of the book, of over-rationalising,
in short, but I do feel that the book would be better if
its internal logic was more clear and its action more
pronounced. I wonder if you feel able to consider these
points and let us know whether you think there is any
substance in them, and, if so, whether any revisions to
the book could be made.

Anna replied on 12th April:

I wish I knew how to make the book more acceptable.
When I started writing, I saw the story as one of those
recurring dreams (hence the repetitive voyages etc.)
which at times become nightmare. This dreamlike
atmosphere is the essence of the whole concept.
Without it, the book would be meaningless. It is an
effect very easily damaged or lost altogether, which
makes me rather nervous about revision. I wish I could
see how this could be done.
    In saying that the pursuit is too endless and drifting,

you seem to be objecting to the book as a whole, since the pursuit *is* the book. The girl's importance as a victim should be enough to justify the pursuing. I mean that peculiar attraction between victim and victimiser, drawing two opposite poles together until finally they are almost identified with one another. This should become clear through all she says and does, as well as what happens to her, inferred rather than stated directly. I feel direct characterisation would be out of place here and would upset the interpersonal balance between the characters.

When you say that you hope for some dramatic incident I am puzzled. I thought the book was full of dramatic incidents with all those fights, shootings, escapes and so on. How could I make the action more pronounced? The book consists of action, doesn't it? I'm not sure what you mean by its internal logic. As I've said, this is not realistic writing. It is meant to be a fantasy or a dream, and dreams are not logical; that's what makes them strange and fascinating (frightening too). To me the characters are very real, so it's hard for me to see why you find them so nebulous and unsatisfactory.

The book underwent a fair number of revisions over the next six months and, on 17th November, Anna submitted a new version of the novel, now titled *The Ice World*, to Peter Owen. On 28th December Owen sent a letter of acceptance, a contract and some suggestions for minor cuts. He was also unhappy about the title, since his firm had recently published a book called *The Ice Palace* (by the Norwegian writer Tarjei Vesaas), and asked Anna whether she could come up with another title. She replied on 30th December:

The best idea I can produce for another title is *Ice*. One

syllable words make effective titles I think. (e.g. *Out*, which everyone seems to think good.) I hope you will agree to this. I prefer it to *The Pursuit, Caught,* and other titles, which to me suggest the activities of real people in a factual novel, because my story is a fantasy and that is the aspect of it I want to accent.

Though the book may be fantasy, its flight takes off from an identifiable situation and set of circumstances: the collapse of the marriage of Stuart and Helen Edmonds, and Helen's global wanderings between 1939 and 1942 against the backdrop of the Second World War, during which time Helen assumed the identity of Anna Kavan. There is little doubt as to the identity of the white-haired girl whom the anonymous pursuer is driving to meet as the book opens:

> I had been infatuated with her at one time, had intended to marry her. Ironically, my aim then had been to shield her from the callousness of the world, which her timidity and fragility seemed to invite. She was over-sensitive, highly-strung, afraid of people and life; her personality had been damaged by a sadistic mother who kept her in a permanent state of frightened subjection.

Nor is there doubt as to the identity of the husband she leaves:

> He was a painter, not serious, a dilettante; one of those people who always have plenty of money without appearing to do any work. Possibly he had a private income: but I suspected him to be something other than what he seemed.

The girl leaves her husband, and the pursuer follows her to a country which is, and is not, Norway; to a town which, with its fortified waterfront, is, and is not Oslo, the first step in Helen Ferguson's wartime journey. It may not be too fanciful to detect elements of Donald Ferguson in the bullying, sadistic character of the warden, under whose domination she falls.

The realistic element of the novel soon evaporates as its action moves to some unspecified tropical location. The Madagascan Indris, who 'flit through the chilly pages of *Ice*', had a rather mundane genesis in one of David Attenborough's natural history programmes which Anna Kavan had seen on television. Intrigued by their vegetarian, pacific natures, she had written to her friend, the American traveller and author, Emily Hahn, to glean further information, explaining that, though she wrote fiction, she did like to get her facts right. Emily Hahn gave two detailed replies and Anna wrote to thank her on 10th March 1964. Dr Bluth had just died, an event that coincided with her completion of the first draft of the book which was to become *Ice*.

The prevailing scenario of apocalypse during the early sixties was that of nuclear destruction, and it is suggested that this was the cause of the catastrophe. Nuclear testing on both sides of the Iron Curtain was then uncontrolled, and for a time both sides vied to test weapons of greater magnitude than the other. Newspapers regularly reported increases in strontium 90 levels, rumours abounded of a 'Doomsday Machine' which would obliterate the planet in the event of nuclear war, and the Cuban missile crisis had served to unearth a terror that had lain barely submerged in the collective psyche for almost two decades. Yet the precise nature of the apocalypse is never clearly drawn by Anna Kavan: it is as if she realized that nuclear terrors might one day be superseded by other nightmares of mass destruction.

The ice which is the agent of destruction had been a threat ever since her childhood when Anna, or rather Helen, was 'taken to a place where there was nothing but snow and ice'. Living in New Zealand Anna had often pondered on the

The Cold World into Ice

proximity of the glacial mass of Antarctica. Some readers of the book have identified it as a correlative of her heroin addiction, and it is a matter of medical fact that addicts detest the cold. Two of the earlier symptoms of withdrawal are cold flushes and shivering: it is not called 'cold turkey' lightly.

The most distinguishable literary influence on the book is Robbe-Grillet and his theories of the *nouveau roman*: in its rejection of character, plot, conventions of geography and chronology, and its sense of an indifferent world. However, Anna Kavan's writing had tended towards this before the *nouveau roman* appeared on the scene. Her enthusiasm for this school, the only group of writers to whom she ever expressed a partiality, was almost certainly because they moved in areas she had already explored.

When Brian Aldiss nominated the book as Best Science Fiction Novel of 1967, he was unaware that Anna both knew and admired his work. 'I simply can't wait to tell you that Brian Aldiss, whom I admire so much, has chosen *Ice* as the best SF book of the year. I'm not making it up. He doesn't know I'm a fan of his either. Can you beat it?' she wrote to Raymond Marriott.

During the sixties the genre of SF responded to the reality of space travel with a movement among its advanced practitioners to explore 'inner space'. There was an attempt, yet to impinge far on public consciousness, to redesignate SF as speculative fiction rather than science fiction. The writer who, in a series of books from *The Drowned World* (1962) to *The Crystal World* (1966), came closest to Anna Kavan in depicting a post-apocalypse landscape was J.G. Ballard. In the last-named book, his vision of the Florida Everglades crystallized by extraterrestrial influences was directly inspired by experimentation with LSD. Quite when Anna took LSD is not known, nor is it clear whether the experience had any influence on those passages of *Ice* that depict the apocalypse in clearly hallucinogenic terms:

I thought of the ice moving across the world, casting its shadow of creeping death. Ice cliffs boomed in my dreams, indescribable explosions thundered and boomed, icebergs crashed, hurled huge boulders into the sky like rockets. Dazzling ice stars bombarded the world with rays, which splintered and penetrated the earth, filling earth's core with their deadly coldness, reinforcing the cold of the advancing ice. And always, on the surface, the indestructible ice-mass was moving forward, implacably destroying all life. I felt a fearful sense of pressure and urgency, there was no time to lose, I was wasting time; it was a race between me and the ice. Her albino hair illuminated my dreams, shining brighter than moonlight. I saw the dead moon dance over the icebergs, as it would at the end of our world, while she watched from the tent of her glittering hair.

The hallucinatory quality of such writing was not lost on the new, principally young, readership who discovered Anna Kavan through the book. She became, in the words of one critic, 'something of a saint to the drug culture'.

As Brian Aldiss admitted, ultimately the book was not really SF, neither speculative nor science. It was *sui generis*, a work in which Anna Kavan had accumulated all of the strengths of her previous fictions and purged their weaknesses, the solipsism and lapses into self-pity, to transcend the boundaries of genre. She had written a metaphysical thriller and this, in such books as John Fowles's *The Magus*, in certain of the belatedly discovered novels of Herman Hesse, even, on a popular level, in Patrick McGoohan's *The Prisoner*, was set to be one of the more compelling forms which the sixties, not a vintage literary decade, was to generate or rediscover. After a career spent mostly out of step with literary trends, Anna Kavan had finally synchronized with the spirit of the times.

17

Fame

*

By the time that Anna Kavan found her audience she was no
longer fit, either physically or mentally, to appreciate the
celebrity that had long eluded her. Shortly after the publication of *Ice* she was profiled in the September 1967 edition of
Nova by Dom Moraes, an Indian-born poet who had also
achieved some fashionable success in the fifties and sixties.
Though the two women did not meet, the profile sat alongside
one of Jean Rhys: both examples of 'great success and long
obscurity'. Anna was in a vacant and pensive mood, with
Peter Owen doing most of the talking as the interview shifted
from her house to the Chanterelle restaurant where, according
to Dom Moraes, 'his authoress turned to me and with her first
audible remark for some two hours, said "I haven't felt anything for twenty years"'.

The photographic contacts were returned to the magazine
marked and gummed together with orange lipstick. Her
always unpredictable behaviour worsened. 'In the world of
reality her social conduct was apt to become erratic, passing
too swiftly from the most delicate perception of a guest's
mood to hurling a roast fowl across the table at him, then
retiring to her bazooka and shortly afterwards be discovered
on her bed reading a novel and eating chocolates out of a box,'
Rhys Davies recalls. It is some evidence of his patience that
Rhys Davies does not record that the target of this outburst
was none other than himself. Perhaps this was the occasion
when, his patience tried to the limit, he remarked to his

brother: 'She's really gone too far this time.'

During the last year of her life Anna increased her use of heroin alarmingly, to the point at which she needed an injection every three hours. Changes in government policy had meant that, in February 1968, Kavan was assigned to an addiction unit, run by a woman who, as this clipping found among her papers indicates, was out of sympathy with Anna's resigned acceptance of her own addiction:

The addiction clinic of Charing Cross Hospital, in Central London, lives in a shop across the street from the back entrance to the hospital proper. A plastic sign by the door identifies it as the hospital's 'psychiatric unit annexe'. Within the clinic is a puzzle box of partitions and tiny offices. Gisella Brigitte Oppenheim, director of the clinic since it opened in February 1968, is a briskly sensible psychiatrist, somewhat of the pull-yourself-together-man persuasion. On the spectrum of English clinic opinion, Dr Oppenheim is known to be generally opposed to prescribing heroin.

'I haven't prescribed heroin for a new patient in three years,' she said. 'Most who come in to the clinic are poly-drug abusers, and settle for methadone. On heroin, it's much more difficult for them to function in the community. Currently we have only two patients left who are on heroin only. And they are *chaotic*: it's a full-time job for an addict to be on heroin; injections are necessary every four to six hours, and in their condition, they can take anywhere from twenty minutes to an hour just to get a fix organised.'

'When we started,' Dr Oppenheim continued, 'our brief from the Ministry of Health supposedly was, "You maintain the addicts until they are motivated to go into hospital to get off drugs." But when we started we had no inpatient facilities; we were obliged from the

beginning to work in a way that would get our patients
into condition to function in the community. In our
experience, many addicts who are detoxified as
inpatients go back on drugs when they get back into
the community. If we had an inpatient unit now, we
wouldn't know what to do with it. Sixty-five percent of
our current attenders (that's sixty-seven out of ninety-
five) are gainfully employed – some work as labourers,
one is a teacher, several have gone back to their
university courses. They can be so stable that nobody
would ever guess they were addicts. Once they are
working, once they have got other interests, personal
relationships, they get fed up with the drug life. It isn't
a conscious decision; it just happens. In many cases,
we can't explain just how and when this point is
reached – certainly it's nonsense for the doctor to claim
the credit.

'Our psychiatric approach is supportive and not
analytical – perhaps, in American terms,
nonpsychiatric. We have two full-time social workers.
The addicts get a great deal of help with simple
practical matters – accommodation, food. The
important thing is to teach them that there is an
alternative to the way they were living when they first
came in. We want them to mix with non-addicts. It is
very important to have their leisure time organised. We
often find that the addict makes a complete break with
the drug-taking group that he has been involved with
before he is able to kick the drug habit.'

Few of these strictures would have applied to Anna Kavan.
She had never consorted with other addicts: her habit was,
like so much in her life, a solitary isolating practice rather
than an entrance ticket to a marginal subculture. Ironically,
the most contact she had with that subculture was in the

waiting-room of the clinic. The discovery of methadone as an effective substitute for heroin had revolutionized techniques for facilitating drug withdrawal, but she was now in her middle sixties and in declining health, and had used heroin for forty years, so this was not a path she was inclined to take. As public hysteria over drug use mounted, she found her position increasingly threatened by the 'pull-yourself-together-man' school of thought, and by those who went further and advocated compulsory detoxification. Writing to Raymond Marriott on 29th November 1968 she commented: 'Thank you so much for the needles. I'm sorry you had so much trouble finding them. The entire supply and demand business has gone mad regarding drugs and anything connected with them. It's a conspiracy of course. Oppenheim's at the back of it all.'

There had been other health problems. Early in March 1968 Anna was admitted to St Charles Hospital, to treat an infection resulting from a badly abscessed leg, the result of a careless injection. On 4th March she wrote to Herman Schrijver: 'They told me today that I'd probably have to be here two or three weeks longer – a dismal prospect indeed. I only escape a continuous intravenous drip because that might spread the infection. No luxury such as a telephone, and I'm forbidden to use my radio. The food is utterly repulsive and uneatable, I live on sandwiches brought by kind friends!' It had been a matter of luck that she obtained treatment at all. 'Quite by chance my neighbour saw a piece of paper blowing about in the road on which I'd written, "Doctor, please come in and ring bell", which I'd put on the outside door for my N.H.S. doctor who of course didn't turn up. My neighbour, with remarkable kindness, telephoned to ask if I was all right, I told her the whole story and she recommended her man, a German, who at once sent me here.' With no release date in sight, Anna voluntarily discharged herself at the end of the month.

During her time in hospital Anna Kavan learned that *En-*

counter were to publish two of her stories. However, a book which David Higham, now acting as her literary agent, had submitted to Peter Owen, had been turned down. Owen felt that only half of the book of short stories was up to her standard and urged her to write more to make a complete collection. Though she was having to attend hospital as an out-patient three times a week, she said she would do what she could.

It was during this period, following her treatment for an abscessed leg at St Charles Hospital and during her out-patient treatment for a spinal disorder at Marsden Hospital, that Anna Kavan met Brian Aldiss. Subsequent to his voting *Ice* the Best Science Fiction Novel of 1967, Aldiss had written to Anna asking if they might meet. He found 'a small but smartly dressed woman, limping slightly but agile, lively, solitary, but seemingly not lonely'. Their meeting was a success and Aldiss later contacted his editor at Doubleday, the American firm which had once published, then rejected, Anna, to recommend the novel to them.

On 24th November 1968 Anna replied to a letter from Peter Owen in which he had requested more stories and invited her to a party at which the guest of honour was to be Anaïs Nin, one of Owen's authors and Anna's most staunch admirer among literary critics:

> I am sending you twenty stories and hope you will find enough material there to make up a book. Five you've already seen. I've put them together in the file.
>
> I think I told you that I'm doing an autobiography in the form of short stories with a connecting thread (something like *Asylum Piece* and *The House of Sleep*). But I'd rather keep these separate from the present series, although they are complete in themselves.
>
> . . . I must apologise too for not answering your letter and kind invitation sooner. I hope very much to

come to the party, but could we leave it open, as I still have to go for hospital treatment most days and don't like to commit myself definitely.

She did not attend the party. On 5th December 1968, at the instigation of Raymond Marriott and Rhys Davies, police broke into her flat. They found her body lying across the bed, her head resting on the Chinese lacquered box in which she kept her heroin. She had been dead for at least twenty-four hours.

18

Post Mortem

*

Scotland Yard Drug Squad were summoned to the house, where they found 'enough heroin to kill the whole street', stockpiled in case compulsory detoxification were ever enforced. A post mortem without an inquest revealed the cause of death to be 'fatty myocardial degeneration'. This is a finding often seen in the case of habitual heroin users: it can, however, occur quite naturally. The heart would imperceptibly work less efficiently, resulting in cardiac failure and subsequent death. Part of the post-mortem examination would have included toxicology screening to ascertain drug levels in the body, and there is little chance that a coroner would have certified death from suicide or overdose, since all the evidence pointed to a heart problem.

The mundane fact that Anna Kavan had died from natural causes after a lifetime of addiction and at least half a dozen serious suicide attempts seems to have been difficult for some of her admirers to grasp. Anaïs Nin recorded in her *Journal* that Anna Kavan had died of an overdose, and Brian Aldiss assumed the cause of death to be suicide. As well as the heroin, Rhys Davies and Raymond Marriott found over forty different varieties of lipstick and a series of paintings depicting gruesome executions and people being hung by their entrails. These were so ghastly that, as her executors under the terms of the 1964 will, which had never been altered, they had them destroyed.

The funeral took place later in the month at Golders Green

Crematorium. It was attended by Rhys Davies, Raymond Marriott, Rose Knox-Peebles, Peter Owen, Diana Johns, the bookseller who had introduced Owen to Anna Kavan, and Mrs Theophila Bluth. As the cortège pulled away from the crematorium, the resentment felt by Mrs Bluth towards the woman who for twenty years had exercised an unbreakable hold on her late husband spilled out. 'How cold, how unaffectionate she was,' she said to the shocked Rose Knox-Peebles. The funeral party returned to Hillsleigh Road for a small gathering before dispersal.

With the ill-luck which she believed had dogged her every movement through life, Anna Kavan died at the dawning of what was to become a secure, if cultish, literary reputation. A week after her death Doubleday agreed to publish *Ice* in the United States. Peter Owen published two posthumous volumes, *Julia and the Bazooka* in 1970, and *My Soul in China* in 1975. The first volume consisted of a selection of the loosely autobiographical stories that Kavan had submitted to Peter Owen shortly before her death, edited by Rhys Davies. *My Soul in China* consisted of a novella, as noted earlier, which Rhys Davies edited down from 90,000 to 30,000 words, and nine short stories, less overtly autobiographical than the previous volume.

The year 1975 also saw the publication of *Honeysuckle Girl*, the novel by Rhys Davies based on the collapse of the marriage between Helen Ferguson and Stuart Edmonds. In the decade following her death, almost all of Anna Kavan's books (including Helen Ferguson's *Let Me Alone*, published now under the name of Anna Kavan), were republished by Peter Owen, and they have been kept in print ever since. Editions of Anna Kavan's books have been published in France, Denmark, Holland, Germany, Spain, Italy, Japan, Brazil and Sweden, as well as in the United States. She is particularly highly regarded in France.

Her reputation received a critical boost with the publication of Anaïs Nin's survey, *The Novel of the Future*. She amended a version of her comments to serve as an introduction to *Ice*, which has not, so far, been used:

I have always admired Anna Kavan among the few writers who dared to explore the nocturnal world of our dreams, fantasies and imagination. It takes courage and great skill in expression. As the events of the world prove the constancy of irrationalism, it becomes absurd to treat such events with rational logic. But people prefer to accept the notion of the absurd rather than to search for the meaning, the symbolic act which is quite clear in whoever is willing to decipher the unconscious. R.D. Laing writes in *The Politics of Experience*: 'We all live in the hope that authentic meetings between human beings can still occur. Psychotherapy consists in the paring away of all that stands between us, the props, masks, roles, lies, defences, anxieties, projections and introjections, in short all the carry-over from the past. Transference and countertransference that we use by habit and collusion, wittingly or unwittingly, as our currency for relationship.'

The writer who follows the designs and patterns of the unconscious achieves the same revelation. From the very first Anna Kavan went into this realm with *The House of Sleep* (a significant beginning), then with a classic equal to the work of Kafka titled *Asylum Piece*, in which the non-rational human beings caught in a web of unreality still struggle to maintain a dialogue with those who cannot understand them. In later books the waking dreamers no longer try: they simply tell of their adventures. They live in solitude with their shadows, hallucinations, prophecies. We admire the deep sea divers exploring the depths of the sea. We do not admire enough those who are able to describe their

151

nocturnal experiences, those who demonstrate that the surface does not contain a key to authentic experience, that the truth lies in what we *feel* and not what we see, or how we see it. Familiarity with inner landscapes would in the end illume the mysteries of the human mind. The scientist can report psychological findings but *the writer has been there*. His is a first hand report. And this is not a personal, unique voyage to the antipodes of the mind – the unconscious is a universal ocean in which all of us have roots.

An elegantly composed and elegiac introduction by Brian Aldiss prefaced the first paperback edition of *Ice* in Great Britain. When, in *Trillion Year Spree*, the practitioner of science fiction became its most authoritative historian to date, he paid Kavan a fulsome, if occasionally inaccurate compliment:

> . . . One such was a woman who, like Mary Shelley, wrote science fiction without knowing it and, in doing so, created one of the great science fiction novels. . . .
> . . . Anna Kavan's story has been told already – how she too was monstrous, how she had the heroin habit for several decades and came to terms with it, and how she committed suicide one week before the news arrived of *Ice*'s acceptance by Doubleday. The story of *Ice* in many ways bodies forth Kavan's inner life. It is the ultimate in catastrophe – the advance of the ice is real enough but it is also the ice of the soul, the heroin encroaching, the habit of death you can't kick. In this sense *Ice* represents one of the high points of science fiction, and so becomes unclassifiable. . . .
> . . . Some of *Ice*'s illustrious relations are clear. Kafka for a start. Anna Kavan's assumed name began with a K in his honour. There is also a surrealist vein,

as exhibited in some of Cocteau's work and in the
painter De Chirico's only novel, *Hebdomeros*. Again,
Ice is a catastrophe novel which goes as far beyond
Ballard as Ballard is beyond Wyndham, sailing into the
chilly air of metaphysics. It looks sideways at its great
contemporary among pornographic novels, Pauline
Reage's *Story of O*. Even more, it is its own self,
mysterious, in some ways unsatisfactory, an enigma –
like all the greatest science fiction, approaching
despair; but, in its acceptance of the insoluble, also full
of a blind force much like hope.

As in our inner beings, there are only three persons
in *Ice*. The pursued and the pursuer often change roles,
become indistinguishable. In that respect, they remind
us how Frankenstein and monster, and their many
later progeny, come to us from the inner being, where
religion, art and science all begin.

The Welsh writer Glyn Jones recalls meeting Rhys Davies a
month after Anna Kavan's death and finding him 'still shattered' by the event, even though Anna had been living pre-
cariously, one day at a time, for as long as he had known her.
In the months after her death figures from Anna's past contacted Davies, some more welcome than others. Agents acting
for Hugh Tevis wrote from South Africa and demanded re-
payment of several months of her allowance which had been
paid after her death. More surprisingly Rhys Davies was contacted by Phyllis Morris, Anna's friend and the former mistress of Stuart Edmonds, who is mentioned in passing in the
diaries of the mid-twenties. Now living in Rome, she revealed
that she had been a school-friend of Anna's, a fact that gives
some clue about how Helen Ferguson and Stuart Edmonds
first met. She also said that it was a nurse who, when Anna
had fallen sick, had given her the first shot of heroin. It would
seem likely that this was so and, having discovered the effect

of the drug, she then sought it on the black market. At the time that the diaries were written, Helen was evidently undergoing medical treatment, and was taking pain-killers and sleeping-pills as well as heroin.

When Anna Kavan's estate was finally settled in March 1969, its net value amounted to £9,246. There was insufficient money to retain Hillsleigh Road, and it was subsequently sold. The paintings were mostly dispersed among friends, as were a few mementoes. When her ashes were forwarded from the crematorium, they were buried in the garden which she loved, beneath a laurel tree.

19

Coda

*

The garden of 19 Hillsleigh Road has been cut back to an approximation of a normal English garden. One could no longer half expect a leopard to emerge from its foliage, least of all in the dead of winter. Her flat has been let: its tenant was both ignorant of and intrigued by the unusual history of the house, and the macabre detail that the earthly remains of its designer lay buried in the grounds.

A freezing fog hung over London and I remembered how, on my first visit to Tulsa, such a fog had hung over that city for my entire stay. It seemed that only the mad, the destitute and visiting researchers walked in Tulsa. I plodded daily through the mist from my stark YMCA room with its near-defunct television capable of receiving only twenty-four-hour Bible stations to the McFarlin Library and the Kavan papers. I remembered meeting a graduate student who had been working for four years on the papers but had still not committed a word to paper. 'Her inner world terrifies me,' she said. The deeper I dug, the more I understood her trepidation.

'Real life is a hateful and tiresome dream,' Anna had written in her 1926 diaries. In 1965 she had written to Raymond Marriott: 'I'm sorry you were so depressed last night. But I'm afraid there's no consolation. Life is just a nightmare and the universe has no meaning. Depression is as good an introduction to oblivion as any other.' Nearly forty years separated the statements, years which she had lived by these convictions.

Both Anna Kavan and her surviving friends blamed her

psychological frailty squarely on her mother. In fairness to the shade of Helen Eliza Bright, this may not be the entire truth, nor does it square with biographical facts. As I said earlier on, Helen Woods was given an allowance of £600 a year at the age of eighteen, equivalent to about £30,000 today, and one which would have allowed her a considerable degree of independence. During the diary years she made numerous comments on her mother's kindness. Her mother encouraged her to go and study art in Dresden. She supported her in her wish to marry or live with Stuart Edmonds. During the late forties, Anna made three visits to her mother in South Africa. Though there may have been financial motives behind these, they did not take place under duress. Far from wishing to be rid of her, her mother wanted her to settle in South Africa. It was her mother who picked up sanatorium bills, and who frequently sent her money when times were hard.

Anna's childhood had not been idyllic, but it differed only in a mild degree from those experienced by other children of her class. 'Many people have unpleasant childhoods. Some survive them and some don't. Anna didn't,' Raymond Marriott commented. The question remains: why did she fail to survive hers?

Helen Woods was the child of Helen Eliza Bright. There are too many similarities between mother and daughter to refute the suggestion that, to a large extent, the daughter's hatred of her mother was not the rage of Caliban at seeing his face in the glass. Though Anna Kavan railed against her upbringing, all the evidence suggests that she treated her son with the same degree of distance. During the diary years he was farmed out to a nurse, as she had been. Photographs indicate that he saw something of his mother while she was living with Edmonds, but she travelled a great deal during these years and their meetings could not have been frequent. And there is the chilling way in which she describes the death of her daughter. Anna Kavan certainly did not like children, detested childbirth and, increasingly, the act of sex. Her mother took a homosexual for a husband: Anna chose to surround herself with an almost entirely homosexual court. She accused her mother of vanity – she who possessed forty different varieties of lipstick and wardrobes full of expensive clothes, who spent hours looking at herself in mirrors. In the mid-sixties Peter Owen had suggested that she apply for an Arts Council bursary and obtained the necessary forms. Anna did not fill them in because she would have had to reveal her true age.

She was certainly partly Helen Eliza Bright, but she was also partly Claude Woods. The traumatic effect of his suicide on the fourteen-year-old Helen Woods was compounded by the fact that she had inherited his depressive temperament. All the psychological evidence points to some manic-depressive condition, almost certainly genetically inherited from her father. Theophila Bluth's statement that Anna was an 'obsessional suicide' is meaningless: suicide by its nature is singular and terminal. For most of her life Anna Kavan had the wherewithal to effect one of the most painless exits from the world known to pharmacology: namely to give herself a massive heroin overdose. When someone fails at suicide on six occasions, the conclusion that they never intended to succeed is inescapable. Like Graham Greene's juvenile toying with Russian roulette, her 'attempts' were devices to make the world more bearable.

For most people the passage of time alleviates the pain of past events. It was not so for Anna Kavan. So the bumbling husband portrayed in *Let Me Alone* changed into the sinister sadist of *Who Are You?*. The break-up of her marriage to Edmonds was sufficiently distressing to prompt a suicide attempt at the time yet, in retrospect, he became the drunken, slobbish Oblomov. Similarly, her mother became 'sadistic', despite the fact that it is somewhat incompatible to complain of neglect from the attentions of a sadist. Anna truly did look back in anger and the past became more nightmarish the further it receded.

Anna Kavan believed that she had been cursed, but the curse came more from her father's genetic inheritance than from her mother's alleged neglect. Rhys Davies, who knew Anna as well as anyone and whose novels are extremely perceptive regarding female psychology, once, in a letter to Herman Schrijver, described Anna's feelings towards her mother as 'love-hate'. Schrijver, who knew both mother and daughter, remarked that 'hate-hate' was nearer the mark, and went on to compare Anna unfavourably with his friend Nancy Cunard. She too had broken with her mother and in doing so had rejected a large maternal inheritance, while Anna, still railing against her mother, accepted money from her. And the painting still remained, looking down on the daughter at work.

Anna was born at a time when her psychological condition was barely recognized, let alone treatable. Sherlock Holmes in fiction and Sigmund Freud in actuality both recognized the utility of cocaine in combating depression. So Anna used cocaine, until an injection of heroin from a nurse demonstrated that it was more effective in blotting out the world. Recreational usage seems a poor phrase to describe her progress towards addiction: attempted self-medication might be more appropriate.

Though she was untypical of an addict in many ways, the path she entered in the mid-twenties was to be trodden by millions during the course of the twentieth century as a small, largely upper-class vice expanded to a global network of supply and demand. Unlike William Burroughs, the other great cartographer of the inner landscape of addiction, she did not dwell on the mechanics of her condition. Heroin apart, she and Burroughs had only this in common: both were in receipt of private incomes and both could, and did, fall back on vast family wealth when the chips were down. Anyone tempted by their literary success and relative longevity to follow the same road should bear this in mind.

That Anna Kavan survived so long was miracle enough, for even suicide attempts programmed to fail may accidentally succeed. Rhys Davies found her battle with despair heroic, a quality that led him to overlook her social transgressions. 'She did not know, and would not accept when told, that courage was giving her a degree of triumph,' he wrote. From that struggle came the books, slim, bleak, appreciated by only a few; a modernist house in a well-to-do suburb of London; some paintings largely scattered among old friends, memories, questions; a garden once lovingly tended surrounded by a high wall, wreathed in a freezing fog which obstinately refuses to lift.

Bibliography

*

Helen Ferguson

A Charmed Circle. London: Jonathan Cape, 1929
The Dark Sisters. London: Jonathan Cape, 1930
Let Me Alone. London: Jonathan Cape, 1930
A Stranger Still. London: John Lane, 1935
Goose Cross. London: John Lane, 1936
Rich Get Rich. London: John Lane, 1937

Anna Kavan

Asylum Piece and Other Stories. London: Jonathan Cape, 1940
Change the Name. London: Jonathan Cape, 1941
I Am Lazarus: Short Stories. London: Jonathan Cape, 1945
Sleep Has His House. London: Cassell, 1948
The Horse's Tale (with K.T. Bluth). London: Gaberbocchus Press, 1949.
A Scarcity of Love. Southport, Lancs.: Angus Downie, 1956
Eagles' Nest. London: Peter Owen, 1957
A Bright Green Field. London: Peter Owen, 1958
Who Are You?. Lowestoft, Suffolk: Scorpion Press, 1963
Ice. London: Peter Owen, 1967
Julia and the Bazooka and Other Stories (with an Introduction by Rhys Davies). London: Peter Owen, 1970
My Soul in China: A Novella and Stories (with an Introduction by Rhys Davies). London: Peter Owen, 1975

Bibliography

There was posthumous republication of *A Scarcity of Love* (1971), *Asylum Piece* (1972), *Sleep Has His House* (1973), *Who Are You?* (1975), *Eagles' Nest* (1976), and *I Am Lazarus* (1978), all by Peter Owen, who also reprinted *Let Me Alone* (1974) by Helen Ferguson, under the name of Anna Kavan.

Literary Criticism

Thus far, published criticism of Anna Kavan's work is largely confined to:

Brian W. Aldiss. *Trillion Year Spree* (with David Wingrove). London: Gollancz, 1986

Anaïs Nin. *The Novel of the Future*. London: Peter Owen, 1969

Reviews and Articles

A selection of important reviews of, and articles on, Anna Kavan:

Rhys Davies. 'Anna Kavan', *Books and Bookmen* (March 1971), 7–10

Max Egremont. 'The Twilight of Anna Kavan', *Books and Bookmen* (June 1978), 43–4

Janice Elliott. 'Drifting Victim', *Sunday Telegraph* (8th March 1970)

Duncan Fallowell. 'Anima and Enema', *The Spectator* (31st January, 1976), 16–17

Vivian Gornick. 'The Great Depression of Anna Kavan'. *The Village Voice* 2–8 December 1981), 49–51, 113

Clive Jordan. 'Icy Heroin'. *New Statesman* (6th March 1970)

——. 'Among the Lost Things', *Daily Telegraph Magazine* (25th February 1972), 39–40, 42, 46

Desmond MacCarthy. 'On Reading Fiction: *I Am Lazarus*, by Anna Kavan', *New Statesman* (1946)

Dom Moraes. 'Anna Kavan', *Nova* (September 1967), 45

Edwin Muir, 'Among the Lost: *A Scarcity of Love* by Anna Kavan', *Sunday Times* (22nd July 1956)

Joyce Carol Oates. 'People Have Always Hated Me'. *New York Times Book Review* (2nd June 1980), 14, 30–1

Martin Seymour-Smith. 'Life of Unreality'. *The Scotsman* (25th August 1967)

Bibliography

Other Sources

Anna Kavan's contributions to *Horizon* may be found in: Vol. VIII, No.45 (1943): Vol. IX, No. 50 (1944); Vol. X, No. 59 (1944); Vol. XI, No. 62 (1945); Vol. XIII, No. 73 (1946).

Anna Kavan's papers are divided between the McFarlin Library at the University of Tulsa, Oklahoma, and the Humanities Research Center at the University of Texas, Austin. The former has by far the most important collection, which includes personal correspondence with Raymond Marriott, George Bullock and Dr K.T. Bluth, the diaries, notebooks, paintings, drafts of published and unpublished novels and stories, and a large number of photographs.

The Humanities Research Center holds material from the archive of Peter Owen, including many letters relating to publication, plus sundry correspondence with Gerald Hamilton, John Lehmann and others. My thanks are due to both these institutions for permission to quote material in their possession.

The Rhys Davies papers at the National Library of Wales, Aberystwyth, contain letters from Anna Kavan to Rhys Davies, and references to her in his correspondence with Raymond Marriott and others.

Correspondence with Herman Schrijver and Charles Burkhart is in the possession of Charles Burkhart and is used with his kind permission.

Priscilla Dorr's doctoral dissertation, 'Anna Kavan: A Critical Introduction', was submitted in 1988 to the Graduate School of the University of Tulsa, and is available on demand from University Microfilm International, Ann Arbor, Michigan. She has also written a useful guide to the Kavan papers at Tulsa, published by the McFarlin Library, Tulsa, Oklahoma.

Rhys Davies's novel, *Honeysuckle Girl* (London: Heinemann, 1975), provides a useful, elegantly written and only thinly fictionalized portrayal of the final years of the Edmonds marriage. Davies takes considerable liberties with chronology, however.

John Symonds's *Conversations with Gerald* (London: Duckworth, 1974) deals with Gerald Hamilton at the time that he was Anna Kavan's lodger. Hamilton also wrote two volumes of autobiography, *As Young as Sophocles* (n.d.), and *Mr Norris and I* (1956), which cover the early part of his extraordinary career.

Index

*